Peer Reviewed By

Dr. Charu Smitha (USA)

Dr. Siddhaling Hiremath

Mr. Darshan Patil, MPH

RAPEDEMIC

This book shook me to the core. I have read many writings on sexual violence, but approaching rape as a public health epidemic is both disturbing and necessary. It forces us to think beyond slogans and laws.

-Ananya Sharma – Social Worker

As a medical student, I found the scientific lens very powerful. The "rapedemiological tetrad" helped me see how society, perpetrators, victims, and environment all interact. A very important contribution.

-Rohan Mehta – Medical Student

Heartbreaking yet enlightening. The stories of Nirbhaya, Hyderabad vet, and others remind us why India cannot stay silent anymore. This book is not easy to read, but it's essential.

-Riya Nair – Women's Rights Activist

The book is bold, but sometimes too clinical. Comparing rape to diseases made me uncomfortable, though I understand the intention. Still, it is a strong call for change.

-Amitabh Singh – Lawyer

I appreciate how the author dismantles myths like "rape is caused by mental illness" or "clothes provoke men." Very well-researched, and every young adult should read this.

-Neha Kulkarni – Psychology Lecturer

I never thought of sexual violence like epidemiology before. It made me reflect on how our culture, patriarchy, and silence allow predators to thrive.

-Imran Khan – Journalist

Painful but necessary. This is not just a book it is a wake-up alarm. The section on underreporting was particularly eye-opening.

-Sunita Rao – NGO Volunteer

The book blends science, psychology, and real cases brilliantly. At times it is overwhelming, but that's the reality of the subject.

-Rajesh Iyer – College Professor

The writing style is raw and courageous. I especially liked how it critiques the legal system's failures. It made me angry, but also hopeful for reform.

Meera Das – Literature Student

I felt the book is heavy for casual readers, but for policymakers, doctors, and lawyers it's gold. The solutions proposed are practical if society dares to adopt them.

-Karthik Reddy – Public Policy Researcher

Reading this felt like carrying a wound in my heart. But silence is worse. I respect the author for breaking the silence with evidence and empathy.

-Pooja Bansal – School Teacher

A groundbreaking book that redefines rape as a social disease. It deserves a place in every university syllabus.

-Siddharth Verma – Graduate Reader

Author Bio

Dr Saleem Nadaf

Hails from Mole village of Belgaum district of Karnataka. Studied MBBS, MPH, from Rajiv Gandhi University of health sciences Bangalore ,Diploma in Emergency Medicine ,Healthcare management and analytics from IIM Kozhikode. Certificate in Tropical diseases from Nagasaki University. International MBA and Healthcare and hospital management. NEBOSH,PG Diploma in Industrial Health and Hygiene. 22 years of experience in national and international healthcare. Author of Two books , The white discharge :Private stories of government doctor. [English]/Ladakh diaries [Kannada]. 50 Short stories in Kannada.

RAPEDEMIC

STETHOSCORPION

BRITISH NOBLE PRESS
UK • INDIA • USA

Copyright

This book is a work of non-fiction. Names and identifying details may have been changed to protect

individuals' privacy. The insights, methods, and reflections presented are based on the author's personal

experience in the education field and are intended to offer guidance and inspiration to educators.

Published by British Noble Press

Printed in India

ISBN: [978-93-7315-820-4]

Dedication

This book is dedicated to every child and woman who lost their lives, who suffered, and who were silenced by the ghastly crimes committed by the darkest corners of humanity. To the victims whose stories were never told, whose pain was never acknowledged, and whose justice was never served this work stands as a small tribute to your memory. To those who survived your strength, resilience, and courage are the reason this book exists. I offer my sincere apologies for writing this book so late, and so slowly. The delay was not due to lack of urgency, but the weight of the subject, the emotional toll, and the isolation that came with it. I wish I could have written it sooner. I wish the world had listened earlier. May this book serve as a voice for the voiceless, a mirror to society, and a step toward understanding, healing, and change.

Contents

Foreword **01**
Author's Note **05**
Preface **09**
Introduction **13**

Part One: Foundational Frameworks

Chapter 1: The Unfolding Silence 19
Chapter 2: The Invisible Epidemic: Statistics of Shame 25
Chapter 3: Broken Definitions, A Shadow of Injustice 29
Chapter 4: The Illusion of Illness - Medicalizing Sexual Violence 33
Chapter 5: The reptilian Brain - Echoes from the Attic of Our Being 39

Part Two: Theoretical Foundations

Chapter 6: The Hormonal Symphony of Puberty 47
Chpater 7: Bipedalism and the Shifting Landscape of Attraction 53
Chapter 8: The Body Awakens: Origins of Sexual Signalling 57
Chapter 9: The Body Awakens - Puberty, Desire 61
Chapter 10: The Enduring Drive - Sexuality, Vitality, and the Human Lifespan 65

Chapter 11: The Animalistic Urge vs. Human Complexity 69

Chapter 12: The Dual Evolution of Breasts 73

Chapter 13: Sexual Choices and Differences 77

Chapter 14: Rethinking Perversion 83

Chapter 15: The Shadow of the Mind, Violence Through the Lens of Severe Psychiatric Disorder- 87

Chapter 16: Rape as Social Disease 93

Chapter 17: Understanding Epidemiology 95

Part Three: Comprehensive Problem Analysis

Chapter 18: The Rapedemiological Tetrad 101

Chapter 19: Unmasking the Predator: Characteristics of Male Perpetrators 113

Chapter 20: The Shadow of the Screen: Porno Factor 125

Chapter 21: The Shadow of the Screen 131

Chapter 22: The Socialization of Pornography: Where Reel Life Warps Reality 137

Chapter 23: Wild Web of Personal Pornography 143

Chapter 24: Deconstructing the Offender 147

Chapter 25: The Shadowed Paths: The Genesis 151

Chapter 26: The Gazelle and the Gathering 157

Part Four: Scope & Impact

Chapter 27: Understanding Child Sexual Abuse 163

Chapter 28: Roots of Rape, Mapping the Conditions That Enable Sexual Violence 169

Chapter 29: The Hidden Numbers, Factors Contributing to Underreporting 173

Chapter 30: The Enduring Scars, Consequences for Survivors 177

Chapter 31: The Societal Fabric of Sexual Violence 181

Chapter 32: Effects of Rape 185

Part Five: System Critiques & Failures

Chapter 33: The Fallacy of Legalized Prostitution as Rape Prevention 191

Chapter 34: The Unprotected: Victim Safety in the Bail System 195

Chapter 35: The Shadow of Accusation 199

Chapter 36: The Siren Song and Unintended Curriculum 205

Chapter 37: The Eroticization of the Everyday and the Erosion of Boundaries 213

Part Six: Solution Frameworks

Chapter 38: Rapist is Killed Long Live the Crime 221

Chapter 39: Reclaiming Safety, Treating Sexual Violence as a Public Health Emergency 223

Chapter 40: The Shadow of Perversion, Parental Roles, Paedophilia, and Child Protection 229

Chapter 41: Strengthening Community Safeguards and Accountability 233

Chapter 42: Bridging the Mental Health Gap: Professionals and Technology 237

Chapter 43: A Medical Perspective on Prevention 243

Refrences For Further Studying **247**

Acknowledgement **251**

Foreword

Dr. Saleem is one of the best authors and I am associated with, since a decade; we share many things in common and discuss many aspects of life. He is admired for his realistic and complete experiences as a person. After reading his book titled 'The White Discharge-Private Stories of a Government Doctor', which unravelled his life experiences and I recommend that everyone should read that book. His present book which deals with burning issue of Rape, sexual assault and murder opens new paradigms to the perspective of the contemporary world. In this book Dr. Saleem presents a detailed factor and reasons which causes to lie behind the current situation. He sheds enormous light on collective psyche, society, Law system and current political aspects and how they are promoting the heinous crimes including rape, murder and sexual assault.

Sex is a very powerful energy like water and fire; we can flourish if it is utilized properly. The same energy can be used in three ways viz, sublimation, use and abuse, when it is sublimated one can achieve Greate things in life primarily, many sublimated the energy of sex and achieved great steps in the social ladder like scientists, spiritual leaders, artist so on. Stalwarts like Swami Vivekananda, Abdul Kalam, Edvard Munch and many more in the pipeline. Secondly, When the same energy is used properly and channelised, one can lead civilised and moral life and it helps to increase the efficiency of a family. The same served the purpose for innumerable ancient Indian writer and theorist Vātsyāyana in his book Kamasutra to understand love, sexuality and relationship. Finally, when it is abused and just let it go it may lead to misery and finally leads to rape.

Ancient Yogis and rishis always suggested to control all the senses and achieve the highest in the life, the highest purpose of life according to Indian culture is liberation (Moksha) which can be achieved through jnana, control of senses (indriyanigraha) sacrifice or limited use of worldly pleasures like sex, food, wealth so on. In ancient Indian scriptures mentioned some practices which helps to control mind viz., yoga, meditation, recitation etc., Because a Sanskrit verse says that eating, sleeping, fearing, and mating are common to both animals and humans but what makes sets human apart is wisdom (jñāna). Without jnana, a human is no better than an animal. To achieve the same one must try not to indulge in worldly pleasures. Another Sanskrit subhāṣita (saying).

Mātā svasrā duhitar vā naika-śayyāsanaṁ bhavet,

Balavān indriya-grāmo vidvāṁsam api karṣati.

This emphasizes the importance of self-restraint and the potential power of the senses (indriyas). Even a wise or learned person (vidvān) may lose control if exposed to tempting situations. Hence, the verse gives a strong warning to maintain proper boundaries, even in close familial relationships, to preserve inner discipline and purity. One of the perspectives of the modern psychology a psychodynamic theory rooted in Freud's theories asserts behaviour is motivated by unconscious process, childhood experiences, instinctual drives, Eros (Life), Thanatos (Death) so on, and human beings are basically a slave of internal conflicts.

Whereas another field of modern psychology a positive psychology is contrary to the others perspectives of psychology viz., psychodynamic, behaviouristic, cognitive, biological so on, it asserts human beings are basically good in nature it is a scientific approach to studying human thoughts, feelings, and behavior, with a focus on strengths instead of weaknesses, building the good in life instead of repairing the bad, and taking the lives of average people up to "great" instead of focusing solely on moving those who are struggling up to "normal" (Peterson, 2008). But it is like the story of five blind men explaining elephant story. All perspectives are equally important to understanding and changing the human behavior.

Dr. Siddalngayya Hiremath
Former Assistant Professor
Department of Clinical Psychology
Manipal College of Health Professions
Manipal Academy of Higher Education MAHE.
+9198866 32882
Siddarth.hiremath@gmail.com

Author's Note

This book is the result of a long, difficult, and deeply personal journey one that began not with a desire to write, but with a need to understand. As a human being, I've often been struck by the paradox of our existence: we are animals, yet we live by the brain. Our thinking mind, our speech, our dexterity, our desires they elevate us, but they also complicate our lives in ways that no other species experiences.

Animals live by necessity. They do not seek comfort in beds, nor do they crave gourmet meals or emotional validation. Their lives are simple, purposeful, and instinctual. Humans, on the other hand, have created layers upon layers of complexity societies, religions, ideologies, and systems of pleasure and pain. Among these, sexual behavior stands out as one of the most misunderstood and misused aspects of human life.

Unlike animals, for whom sex is purely reproductive, humans have turned it into a multifaceted act of pleasure, dominance, revenge, frustration, and sometimes, violence. The act of rape, in particular, is not just a crime of lust; it is a manifestation of deeper psychological, social, and emotional dysfunctions. And yet, society often refuses to confront this reality.

During the COVID-19 lockdown a time when the world was forced into introspection I found myself disturbed by the continued reports of sexual violence. The brutality did not pause. If anything, it revealed the darker corners of human nature. That period became the turning point for me. I began researching, reading, and reflecting. I waited for someone to write the book I was hoping to read. No one did. So I decided I must.

One of the most startling discoveries in my research was Paul Smithyman's The Undetected Rapist, a work that invited anonymous confessions from perpetrators who had escaped legal consequences. It was controversial, unsettling, and yet, it opened a window into the psychology of those who commit such crimes. It made me realize that understanding the mind of a rapist is not about sympathy it's about prevention. If even one life can be saved through early psychological intervention, then this work is justified.

Over six years of research, I faced rejection, isolation, and judgment. Friends distanced themselves. Colleagues refused to engage. Even the presence of a folder named "Rape" on my desktop drew suspicion and discomfort. But every silence, every refusal, became part of the data evidence of how society avoids confronting uncomfortable truths. Some people refused to review my work on pornography. Others agreed, then disappeared. Even my closest friends stopped answering my calls. I had to beg, reassure, and promise anonymity yet many still turned away.

These reactions, though painful, were revealing. They showed me how deeply ingrained our discomfort is with discussing sexual violence. They also strengthened my resolve. I realized that this book was not just necessary it was urgent.

I was advised to make the book less scientific, more accessible to the average reader. I tried, but I may have failed. The book remains rooted in psychology, sociology, anatomy, history, and philosophy. It is not just a book it is a document, a mirror, and a call to action.

This work is not perfect, nor is it complete. I envision it as an open book, one that evolves with time, with contributions from students, psychologists, sociologists, and thinkers. I hope it sparks dialogue, challenges norms, and most importantly, brings change.

To those who refused to speak thank you. Your silence spoke volumes.

To those who supported me, even quietly I am grateful.

And to you, the reader thank you for your courage to read. May this book help us understand, heal, and prevent.

Dr Saleem MPH

Preface

Born out of years of clinical observation, ER visits, and a mounting dissatisfaction with society's insufficient response to one of humanity's most devastating pathologies, this book is an uncomfortable journey into the darkest corners of human behavior. The author felt obliged to approach this crisis from a perspective that has been conspicuously lacking from public discourse: medical science. He has witnessed the immediate aftermath of sexual violence, the mangled bodies, shattered minds, and ruined lives that arrive at hospital doors, because she is a medical professional. Rather than academic theory, the harsh realities of clinical practice served as the inspiration for this work. Every rape kit handled, survivor treated, and family destroyed by sexual assault is evidence of a social disease that requires the same rigorous scientific approach to treatment as other epidemics. Despite decades of legislative changes, public awareness campaigns, and social movements, the prevalence of sexual violence continues to rise, suggesting that fundamental aspects of this phenomenon remain poorly understood.

A simple yet profound realization led to the writing of this manuscript: if traditional approaches to law enforcement, the legal system, and social advocacy have failed to halt this wave of violence, it might be time to apply the same tactics that have been effective in treating other human illnesses. Thanks to medicine, smallpox has been eliminated, tuberculosis has been contained, and cancer has been transformed from a deadly disease to one that can be cured. Instead of morally condemning the infections, these successes were achieved by systematically investigating their mechanisms, determining risk factors, and developing evidence-based treatments. In order to develop a clear enough understanding of the biological, psychological, and social causes of sexual violence to develop effective preventative measures, the author approaches the topic with the same clinical objectivity that is applied to the study of any pathological condition. This point of view may be distressing to those who prefer to view rape as a crime or a moral failing, but discomfort such as this is often the price of scientific progress. Drawing on evolutionary biology, neuropsychology, epidemiology, and clinical psychiatry, this work attempts to create a comprehensive framework for understanding sexual violence as a complex syndrome with identifiable precursors, predictable patterns, and quantifiable outcomes. In an attempt to apply public health approaches to a problem that has traditionally been the purview of criminal justice systems, the "Rapedemiological tetrad",victim vulnerability, perpetrator agency, facilitating environment, and influential factors was introduced.

Those looking for easy solutions or cozy assurances are not the target audience for this book. The systematic study of the social factors that facilitate sexual violence, the candid discussion of victim vulnerability factors, and the clinical investigation of perpetrator psychology will all challenge preconceived notions and possibly elicit strong reactions. However, accurate diagnosis and effective treatment, regardless of how distressing the diagnosis may be, have always been the goals of effective medicine. The dangers of viewing sexual violence through a medical lens are acknowledged by the author. There is a risk that it will seem to medicalize moral responsibility, reduce complicated human experiences to biological processes, or unintentionally support victim-blaming narratives. These concerns are valid and have been carefully considered throughout this work. The greater risk, however, is allowing this epidemic to spread unchecked while society keeps using proven ineffective strategies. Any discomfort that might result from looking at this issue from a different angle is greatly outweighed by the cost of inaction, which is expressed in terms of economic burden, societal dysfunction, and human suffering.

Introduction

This book must be viewed through the rigorous lens of medical science rather than the conventional sociological, criminological, or legal scholarship lenses, as medical professionals witness the horrific outcomes of sexual assault in clinics and emergency rooms worldwide. On the grounds that rape is to be considered what it really is-a pathological deviation growing into an epidemic in human societies-varied disciplines within medical science now study the pathophysiology and epidemiology of diseases that afflict populations. Sexual violence should therefore be subjected to the same kind of scientific scrutiny, void of political rhetoric and moral sentiments that have ever blocked the cognizance of this illness spreading throughout human society. Along with that, the human body formed complicated biological and psychological systems meant to assure survival and procreation. Within this same biological framework, there are also pathways for serious dysfunction. Sexual violence is one such terrible deviation that perverts the very biological impulses that should sustain life and continuity. According to medical professionals, rape is not merely a crime; rather, it is an indication of serious structural defects in the social organism that manifest in individuals whose neurological and psychological composition has been seriously compromised.

Consider the parallels to other diseases. Cancer arises when cellular growth mechanisms that are normally tightly regulated become dysregulated and destructive. Sexual violence also occurs when a complex interplay between social conditioning, neurochemical processes, and evolutionary drives fatally impairs a person's capacity for empathy, impulse control, and respect for their own autonomy. From a medical perspective, it is necessary to investigate the biological underpinnings of human sexual behaviour. The three-brain theory posits that the reptilian brain is a vestige from an evolutionary time when life was rudimentary-the brain giving rise to the basic goals of dominance, reproduction, and survival. In the next level above are limbic structures, which have to do with emotion and memory, which in turn are overseen by the executive functions of the prefrontal cortex: moral reasoning and control. This organization usually fails woefully when it comes to the making of sexual crimes, either because sexual urges overpower higher cognitive functions or because the very presence of developmental trauma has altered these neural pathways in such a way that there is no longer any neurobiological process left for empathy and self-control. A delicate neurochemical dance occurs-the cascades of hormones that teach us sexual behaviour, with testosterone, dopamine, serotonin, and oxytocin as the main players. This system, when disturbed by factors like genetic predisposition, environmental trauma, or substance abuse, may allow extroverted predatory behaviour to creep in. When we understand these intricate processes, our potential solutions for prevention and intervention can be much more successful than those reactive ones currently in place, yet we cannot offer excuses to anyone. From an epidemiological standpoint, there are certain aspects that communicate an analogy between rape and infectious disease outbreaks. It affects certain cohort groups more than others; it tends to cluster in specific geographic locales, is transmitted through particular social networks, and environmental factors pose innumerable risks. The classical epidemiological triad encompassing victim vulnerability, perpetrator agency, facilitating environment, and influential factors finds its reflection in the "Rapedemiological tetrad" suggested by this analysis. Victim vulnerability includes biological, psychological, and social factors that increase the probability of an individual becoming a victim. Like host susceptibility in infectious diseases, this could be neurobiological development based on age, patterns of socialisation aimed at silencing assertiveness, social isolation from protective social networks, and exposure to environmental toxins like drugs or alcohol, all of which can impair one's ability to make decisions or resist physically. The perpetrator agency is a manifestation of the pathological agent; individuals whose psychological makeup has been so altered by the effects of developmental trauma, environmental conditioning, or genetic predisposition that they can seriously harm others.

The facilitating environment includes the physical, social, and cultural elements (e.g. various patriarchal power structures that reinforce male dominance, available substances that disinhibit behaviour, available pornographic images or media that link sexual arousal to violence and degradation, and physical spaces that enable potential victims to not be reached by any protective intervention) that enable sexual violence to occur. To link crime control in all its forms, an example of a broader facilitating environment exists, where pre-existing and/or relevant anthropogenic conditions (grounded by laws, norms, economies, or social solidarity) either facilitate or restrict predatory behaviours from emerging and/or being expressed. This medical model mandates that the simplistic view of moral failings of the individual must be abandoned; sexual violence must be understood as a syndrome based on identifiable risk factors and understood via identifiable progressions, measures, and quantifications of harm. While it is true that sexual violence can never truly be eliminated, but just like we have done with polio and smallpox, we can dramatically minimize it using multi-faceted, evidence-based, and strategic public health interventions that are focused on the biological, psychological, and social determinants of the violence.

The perpetrators of sexual violence are a heterogeneous group of people with pathological characteristics related to severe deficits in empathy development, distorted cognitive schemas of human worth and consent, dis-regulated impulse control, and often past victimization experiences that leave struggling with cycles of violence and trauma. Due to the complex dynamics of genetic vulnerabilities and environmental hardships, these people develop neurobiological impairments and pathological adaptations to unacceptable behaviours in a civilized society. The assessments are that they are more than just "evil" or "immoral." The experience is that we need to completely revolutionize how society responds to sexual violence by shifting from a primary reliance on post-event consequences to including robust identification and intervention strategies at the front end of the violence continuum. In the same way that evidence informs medical practice, as health providers screen for potential risk factors for cancer, and then develop preventive actions, we need processes for identifying those at high risk and engaging them in intensive therapeutic services prior to them contacting society and harming others. Sexual violence is not an unavoidable feature of human society; rather, it is a preventable pathology that can be comprehended, anticipated, and ultimately eliminated by scientific means.

PART I: FOUNDATIONAL FRAMEWORK

Chapter 1

The Unfolding Silence

The air in India is thick, with the weight of centuries of wisdom, contradiction, and quiet suffering. Yet, in recent decades, this air has been ruptured by a different sound: the anguished cry of dignity violated, of lives shattered by sexual violence. These cries are not merely echoes of individual pain; they are the voice of a nation grappling with a crisis that refuses to fade.,.

The name **Nirbhaya** became a symbol of this reckoning. Her brutal gang rape and murder in Delhi in 2012 became a national trauma that transcended the boundaries of a single crime., It forced India to confront its darkest truths. For a moment, it seemed like the country had awakened. Laws were amended, protests surged, and the streets filled with candlelight vigils and slogans demanding justice. But the promise of change proved fragile.

Years later, in **Hyderabad**, a young veterinary doctor was raped, murdered, and her body burned in an act so horrifying it reignited the nation's grief.,. The brutality mirrored Nirbhaya's case, reminding us that the monster had never left. It had simply adapted, grown bolder, more vicious. The veterinarian's case was not an anomaly; it was a continuation.,

Then came the **Kolkata medics case**, where two female doctors were sexually assaulted in a hospital, a place meant for healing. The violation of women within institutions of care and trust underscored a terrifying truth: no space is truly safe. Not homes, not streets, not workplaces, not even hospitals.

These three incidents, are grim milestones in a landscape littered with names like **Unnao, Kathua,** and **Shakti Mills**. Each name represents a life torn apart, a family devastated, and a society that failed to protect. Hundreds of cases are officially recorded each year, but countless others remain buried in silence, hidden by fear, shame, and stigma.

Public response has been intense but inconsistent. Candlelight vigils, once symbols of unity and protest, now flicker against a backdrop of despair. The streets have become stages for grief, rage, and confusion. Demands for justice range from legal reform to brutal retribution. Yet, even in these moments of collective mourning, the rot persists. Women have been molested during protests meant to honour victims. The irony is grotesque., The media, which could have been a force for change, often turns tragedy into spectacle.

Journalists dissect victims' lives while sensationalizing their trauma. Perpetrators receive disturbing fascination, with some achieving notoriety in political and social discourse. Publishers print books, filmmakers produce documentaries, yet violence persists unabated.

One of the most chilling examples is the juvenile rapist in the Nirbhaya case, who walked free after serving a short sentence due to his age. His release was a stark reminder of the gap between legal definitions and the horrifying reality of sexual violence. While some perpetrators have been killed in police encounters, offering momentary catharsis, the crimes have not stopped. In fact, they've grown more brutal: victims have been burned, buried, drowned, mutilated. Each case seems to push the boundaries of cruelty further.

In response, society has offered band-aid solutions: pepper sprays, self-defence classes, mobile apps, helplines. These can be labelled as cures but, they are fragile shields in a collapsing world. Women continue to live in fear, clutching safety as a second skin. India, a country that once celebrated feminine divinity, now finds itself globally shamed for failing to protect its women.

Rape, molestation, and harassment transcend their legal definitions as crimes. They reveal a deeper pathology within our social fabric.

What is rape, fundamentally? It is not sexuality distorted, but power weaponized. It represents the ultimate theft: of bodily autonomy, of human dignity and, of self-determination. The act destroys more than the moment; it fragments identity itself.

This book proposes a radical shift: to explore rape through the **psychic lens**, a deep psychological investigation into the minds of rapists. What turns a seemingly "normal" child into a predator? What societal forces warp empathy into cruelty? Can early behavioural patterns be identified and addressed before they manifest as violence?

This approach treats rape as a **public health crisis, going beyond its legal jurisprudence. Its starks as, a** "non-infective epidemic" that demands urgent, innovative solutions. It calls for prevention, beyond t punishment and urges us to move beyond shame and silence, to confront the crisis with clarity and courage.

Sexual violence has infiltrated every corner of society. From casting couches in Bollywood and Hollywood, to classrooms, religious institutions, gyms, buses, hostels, and homes; no space is untouched.

Trusted figures such as politicians, teachers, and spiritual leaders have crossed boundaries with impunity, and their actions can no longer be dismissed as a collection of isolated horrors, for they reveal instead the presence of a deeper and more pervasive systemic ailment.

The case of **Aruna Shanbaug**, for examples, who lived in a vegetative state for 42 years after a sodomizing assault, is a haunting reminder of the long-term impact of sexual violence. Her suffering was a prolonged assault on human dignity, endured in silence, forgotten by most, and ignored by many.,

In earlier decades, **dowry deaths** filled the headlines, as brides were burned for unmet demands. The violence has not ceased; it has only taken on new forms. Today, India stands condemned on the global stage, branded as one of the most unsafe places for women., Each new case follows a familiar script: delayed police action, political exploitation, fleeting public outrage, and eventual abandonment. Victims' families are often left to fend for themselves, silenced by threats or pressure. Conviction rates remain low. Justice is rare. Silence becomes survival.

Some rapists appear driven by a perverse ambition to surpass previous crimes in brutality, Reports describe genital mutilation, insertion of blades, disembowelment, even blinding victims. These acts of violence are deliberate attempts to strip away humanity itself.,

Do these perpetrators not see the media coverage? Or do they, more disturbingly, find inspiration in it, as, blueprints for depravity?

India, once the land of the **Kama Sutra**, now faces a crisis of sexual violence that threatens its very identity. This is a national emergency, defined by a collapse of empathy, morality, and collective will.,

This chapter marks the beginning of an uncompromising journey. A descent into the unspeakable. But also, a call to action. We can no longer afford denial. The silence has spoken for too long. The time has come to listen to the cries, to trace the scars, to acknowledge the survivors, and to act.

Crime, Terror, Rape: United States Flags India Travel Risks

The US Department of State has continued to issue a Level 2 travel advisory for American nationals living in or traveling to India, urging them to "exercise increased caution" due to ongoing risks linked to crime and terrorism.

Edited by Anushree Jonko World News Jun 25, 2025 15:13 pm IST

Chapter 2

The Invisible Epidemic: Statistics of Shame

Any conversation about sexual violence, especially rape, runs into a major obstacle: we simply do not have reliable numbers. Unlike many other crimes, the true scale of rape is hidden behind silence and broken systems. When we try to measure this trauma, we face a disturbing truth: the official figures, often taken from national crime bureaus, tell only part of the story and almost never the whole one. The reasons for this are many, and each one reveals how deeply flawed our systems of reporting and measurement really are.

The most significant issue is underreporting and non-reporting. The vast majority of rapes never reach the police station. Survivors often carry the brutal weight of silence, shaped by fear of retaliation, shame, stigma, and the very real possibility of being further humiliated by insensitive officials or an unresponsive justice system. Many know that filing a complaint could mean social ostracization or being put on trial themselves, and so they choose to stay quiet, enduring their pain in the shadows.

Even in cases where survivors gather the courage to take a step forward, there are documented instances where police refuse to even register complaints. Sometimes reports are downplayed, sometimes survivors are pressured to withdraw their allegations, and sometimes the crime is dismissed outright. This refusal at the very first point of justice ensures that a disturbing number of cases never enter the official record, leaving an invisible scar on the collective truth of the crime.

Then there is the problem of ambiguous classification. When cases are recorded, they are not always consistent. Labels such as "rape and murder," "attempted rape," or "rape" are used differently across jurisdictions and timeframes. Without clear and standardized categorization, statistics lose their clarity. Numbers get blurred, and what was meant to be evidence becomes an opaque muddle where the true extent of violence is hidden in technicalities.

Another troubling issue is the deliberate manipulation of data. The possibility of fabrication or quiet omission cannot be brushed aside. In some systems, there is immense pressure to keep crime rates looking lower than they are, which means sexual violence is deliberately undercounted. This kind of statistical denial is especially insidious because it gives the illusion of safety where none exists, and it turns survivors' experiences into expendable numbers, erased for the sake of reputations.

All of this makes one thing clear: to rely solely on official figures, such as those provided by the National Crime Records Bureau in India or similar agencies elsewhere, is to fundamentally misunderstand the scale of the problem. These figures are often presented as the hard truth, but in reality, they are a pale shadow of what is happening on the ground. At best, they form a grim baseline, a visible tip of an iceberg whose true size lies hidden beneath the surface. To cite them as definitive is not only misleading but also dangerous, because it risks minimizing the crisis and granting false legitimacy to data that is structurally flawed.

Sexual violence, therefore, cannot be represented by charts alone. It is a crisis that resists quantification, a wound spread far too deep in a society that still finds ways to look away. The absence of trustworthy numbers is not just a statistical problem, but a moral one, reflective of silenced voices and systemic neglect. The violence is pervasive, profound, and for the most part, invisible. Understanding this vacuum, this deliberate and accidental void of data, is crucial to comprehending not only the vulnerability of survivors but also the hypocrisy of societies that preach protection while quietly suppressing the truth. Until we face this invisibility head on, any conversation about rape will remain incomplete.

THE TIME OF INDIA
FEBRUARY 17, 2025
TIMES

Rape cases rose by 8% in 2024; total cases registered went up by 7%: CM

Chapter 3

Broken Definitions, A Shadow of Injustice

"Grabbing breasts, pulling strings of pyjamas not sufficient to hold rape charge," ruled the Allahabad High Court. Justice Ram Manohar Narayan Mishra directed the POCSO court to issue fresh summons under lesser charges, downgrading the act to a minor offense of 'assault or abuse' of a girl.

In the sterile hum of the courtroom, where justice is meant to echo with clarity and conscience, this ruling landed like a thunderclap. The space, heavy with unspoken truths and fragile hope, seemed to tremble under the weight of its own contradictions. Somewhere in that silence, the ghost of **Aruna Shanbaug** lingered, her attacker, the man who sodomized and strangled her with a dog chain, walked free after a short sentence. His crime had slipped through the cracks of a legal system too narrow, too outdated, to name it for what it truly was.

The law, in its current form, often fails to grasp the full horror of sexual violence. It speaks in clinical terms: penetration, intercourse, consent. This reduces the, acts of terror to anatomical checklists. In Aruna's case, sodomy was not even classified as rape. It was a legal footnote: a technicality. The monstrous act that left her in a coma for decades was not enough to meet the legal threshold of "rape" as defined at the time.

The absurdity of such definitions is, is dangerous. Euphemisms like "assault with a friendly weapon" or crude phrases like "crash landing on thigh land" trivialize trauma. They reduce profound suffering to punchlines, but rape is not friendly. It is not trivial. It is a storm of terror, a hurricane of violation that leaves lives in ruins. And yet, the law often treats its components -, intimidation, abduction, assault, as isolated events, failing to see the monstrous whole they form together.

Aruna paid the price for this fragmented understanding, not just once, but every day of her prolonged, silent suffering. Her case is a damning indictment of a legal system that could not name her pain, let alone punish it.

So, what, then, is rape?

The truth is: the law has long struggled to define rape in a way that reflects its reality. But change, though slow, has begun. The whispers of survivors are rising into a collective roar. Legal definitions are being challenged, expanded, rewritten. Sodomy is now recognized as rape. Other forms of assault, once dismissed or ignored, are finally being acknowledged for the deep psychological scars they leave behind.

Yet even as the legal landscape evolves, a deeper question remains: **What drives someone to rape?**

Is it a calculated hunger for power, a need to dominate, humiliate, and destroy? Or is it the sudden eruption of darkness from a fractured mind? The psyche of the rapist remains a murky and neglected terrain, where trauma, pathology, toxic masculinity, and social conditioning collide. Researchers have tried to chart this darkness in the hope that understanding might lead to prevention, but the answers they find are tangled, unsettling, and far from complete.,

The old excuses no longer hold. "She was too beautiful to resist" collapses under the weight of cases involving elderly women and infants. "Her clothes provoked him" disintegrates when one considers the gang rape of a fully clothed nun. These are not crimes of passion. They are crimes of power wherein, brutal assertions of control, often committed by those who feel powerless in other aspects of their lives.

The word "rape" comes from the Latin reparent seize, to carry off. In ancient times, it was how a man claimed a wife: by taking her, violating her, and bringing her back as property. That legacy lingers. Even today, rape is often seen not as a crime against a person, but as a stain on a family's honour, a disruption of social order.

However, rape is not a private shame. It is a public emergency. A **non-infective epidemic.** A psychic malignancy with social vectors, psychological triggers, and generational consequences. It reveals a symptom of a deeper illness in our collective psyche; to confront it, we must move beyond narrow definitions and outdated laws. We must explore the intersection of law, psychology, and culture. We must recognize that rape stems from power, control, and the dehumanization of another person.,.

Only then can we begin to dismantle the structures that enable it. Only then can we hope to build a society where justice transcends courtroom technicalities and becomes a lived reality.

Chapter 4

The Illusion of Illness – Medicalizing Sexual Violence

Framing rape as a "disease" represents a troubling shift in how society attempts to understand sexual violence. This model rests on two key assumptions: first, that perpetrators suffer from a form of mental illness; and second, that their actions stem from uncontrollable sexual impulses that override rational thought. Within this framework, rapists become psychologically 'sick' individuals as victims of their own pathology rather than morally accountable agents,

This perspective places offenders into what sociologists call the "**sick role**", a conceptual space where individuals are presumed to lack control over their behaviour and are expected to seek treatment rather than punishment. Historically, some have viewed rape as an "explosive expression" of internal pressures, not a deliberate act of violence. Psychological tools like the **Minnesota Multiphasic Personality Inventory (MMPI)** have been used to support this view, often highlighting elevated scores on the psychopathic deviate scale.

While it is true that a small number of rapists may suffer from diagnosable psychiatric disorders, just as some thieves or murderers might, empirical research consistently shows that **only about 5%** of men who commit rape are experiencing active psychosis at the time of the assault. Despite this, the belief that rape is inherently linked to mental illness remains popular in certain academic and legal circles.

This focus on individual pathology has serious consequences. It shifts moral and legal responsibility away from the perpetrator and toward an abstract notion of illness. Worse still, some early criminological theories, such as those proposed by **Hans von Hentig**, shifted the lens toward the victim. Von Hentig suggested that some individuals were "born victims," prone to self-harm or victimization, and even proposed that victims might "tempt" their attackers. In cases like incest, he argued, the lines of seduction and responsibility could blur.

This line of thinking was expanded by **Marvin Wolfgang** and **Menachem Amir** in the 1970s. Amir's study introduced the concept of **victim precipitation**, distinguishing between acts of commission (e.g., withdrawing consent or accepting a ride from a stranger) and omission (e.g., not resisting or dressing in a way that supposedly "arouses" the offender). These ideas dangerously imply co-responsibility, distorting the reality of rape as a non-consensual act of domination.

Psychoanalytic literature has further reinforced these problematic narratives. Writers like **Nils Littner** introduced categories such as "true victims" and "professional victims," the latter allegedly possessing unconscious masochistic desires that draw them toward assault. These individuals were described as "cooperating" with their assailants; an idea that would be unthinkable if applied to victims of other violent crimes. Some even claimed that girls who are raped suffer from pre-existing emotional problems that "invite" the assault.

These narratives are ethically flawed and dangerous, they redirect attention from the wilful behaviour of perpetrators to the supposed psychological flaws of victims. They suggest that sexual aggression is an abnormal deviation, rather than a reflection of broader social conditioning. In doing so, they comfort society with the illusion that rapists are rare, broken men, outliers even, rather than products of a culture that normalizes male entitlement and female subordination.

The illusion is, then shattered when viewed through a sociological or anthropological lens. Studies comparing **"rape-prone" and "rape-free" societies** reveal clear patterns: societies with entrenched male dominance, militarism, and rigid gender roles tend to have higher rates of sexual violence. In contrast, societies that value women's reproductive labour and grant them economic and social power experience significantly lower rates of rape.

A consistent finding in anthropological literature is the **inverse relationship between women's economic autonomy and their risk of sexual violence.** Where women have greater control over resources and decision-making, violence against them tends to decrease. Rape, then, cannot be understood in isolation, for, it is shaped by cultural norms, power dynamics, and systemic disenfranchisement.

Feminist scholarship deepens this understanding by showing

how sexual violence functions as a **tool of social control**. In patriarchal systems, rape reinforces gender hierarchies by punishing female autonomy and asserting male dominance. The benefits of this system are not limited to individual rapists but, they extend to men collectively, who continue to occupy positions of power and privilege. This system is upheld by what sociologist J**ean Lipman-Blumen** calls "**control myths**" wherein, deeply internalized beliefs that justify male superiority and female subordination. Two of the most enduring myths are that men are inherently more competent, and that they act in women's best interests.

These myths not only restrict women's access to power but also contribute to a culture of disbelief when they speak out. Victims who come forward are often met with suspicion, forced to defend their own behaviour rather than the actions of their assailants. Meanwhile, the cultural narratives that uphold male entitlement remain largely unchallenged.

By embracing the broader and more uncomfortable truth that rape is shaped both by individual psychology and by societal structures, we begin to see it not as a medical anomaly but as a socially conditioned act of power. The limitations of the disease model become clear when placed alongside the overwhelming influence of cultural norms and institutionalized inequality.

In the next chapter, we will trace the historical emergence of the **"disease model" of rape**, examining the scientific debates that shaped it. We will critically assess the claim that uncontrollable sexual impulses are central to understanding sexual violence, and contrast this with growing evidence that rape is far more often an act of power than pathology. This exploration will take us deeper into the biology of behaviour, forcing us to confront how evolutionary legacies and social systems intersect to produce violence.

Chapter 5

The Reptilian Brain – Echoes from the Attic of Our Being

Our brains as, magnificent in their complexity, stand as a living archive of evolution, constructed layer upon layer through deep time. At the very foundation of this neural architecture lies the ancient **reptilian brain**, the oldest remnant of our biological inheritance. To fully grasp the legacy of this primal core, we must look further back, to a world without brains or eyes, where life first flickered into existence as single-celled organisms.,

These primordial creatures navigated their world not through thought or vision, but through **touch.**

Touch, then, was our first language. These organisms extended pseudopods, or temporary "false feet," into their environment, feeling their way forward through direct contact. , Long before there were words or even conscious thought, there was sensation. In us, their distant descendants, the importance of touch remains undiminished. A breeze against the skin, the warmth of sunlight, and the pressure of a hand are more than sensory inputs; they are echoes of ancient contact, reminders of a time when touch was survival.,

Pleasure, too, has always been intertwined with touch. In moments of sensuality and sexuality, the sense of touch takes on a heightened role, often becoming the primary vehicle of intimacy. Even in darkness, or the anonymity of a crowded room, a deliberate touch can elicit a profound response. For some, this primal connection to tactile sensation becomes an obsession, expressed, at times, in ways society deems perverse. The hand gravitates toward the body's most sensitive zones: buttocks, breasts, neck, stomach, groin. In some cases, the act of touching itself, without penetration or even removal of clothing, can trigger sensations comparable to sexual climax. This power, this proximity of touch to desire, explains its perilous potential, and perhaps, its misuse.

To understand how this sensuality becomes misdirected or weaponized, we must ascend the evolutionary ladder, from the pseudopod to the **triune brain**, a model proposed by neuroscientists, which describes the human brain as composed of three nested structures: the reptilian complex, the limbic system, and the neocortex.

The **reptilian brain**, so named for its resemblance to the brains of reptiles, governs basic functions such as, heartbeat, breathing, arousal, aggression. It's focus lies in basic survival, without regard for ethics, empathy, or long-term consequences. In the lizard or snake, and in our own early ancestors, this brain responded to the world with a limited but essential vocabulary: **eat, mate, sleep**. From this foundation emerged the more emotionally attuned **limbic system** and the rational, planning **neocortex**. But the primitive architecture remains.

This is the neural bedrock upon which all higher cognition rests. It is unthinking but not inactive; a relentless engine of instinct. In this evolutionary view, the **sex drive** is not merely a cultural construct or a romantic yearning, but a biological imperative, alongside hunger and fatigue, libido is embedded as a core survival function. The absence of sexual satisfaction becomes experienced as deprivation rather than mere disappointment

Just as a starving person may steal bread, beg, or fight for sustenance, so too can those driven by unsatisfied sexual urges act in ways that disregard social norms, legal structures, and, most perilously, the boundaries of others. When sexual desire is interpreted through this evolutionary lens, it can appear as something elemental and uncontrollable; a hunger that, if unmet, may lead to what some have dangerously called the **"theft" of intimacy.**

But this analogy, seductive in its simplicity, veers into dangerous territory. It risks **justifying or naturalizing sexual violence** by equating rape with the seeking of food or rest. It also reinforces the idea that sex is a **need**, not a **desire**; a distinction with profound moral and legal implications. Unlike starvation, sexual frustration is not fatal. It is not an emergency requiring resolution at any cost. And yet, when framed through the reptilian logic of the brain, some argue otherwise: that denial of sex can produce desperation, that men are biologically wired to pursue gratification, that violation becomes a tragic but understandable byproduct of evolutionary programming.

This line of thinking resurrects the same problematic assumptions examined in the previous chapter, the idea that rape stems from uncontrollable biological urges, from mental illness, from anything but **choice**. Biology, while powerful, does not determine behaviour. It offers impulses, never instructions. We carry within us the remnants of ancient creatures, yet we are not only reptiles. We are also mammals who feel and humans who think. The neocortex, the outer layer of the brain linked to reasoning, judgment, and empathy, evolved precisely to modulate these base impulses, to evaluate risk, to respect boundaries, and to imagine consequences. In this lies our capacity to override our urges.

The presence of a sex drive does not necessitate its expression through coercion. To suggest otherwise remains scientifically flawed and **ethically corrosive**. It reduces rape to a misfiring of instinct, stripping it of its real character as a **deliberate act rooted in power** rather than passion.,

This is not to deny the reality of sexual frustration, or the role of the body in shaping experience. But the invocation of the reptilian brain as a justification for sexual violence collapses the gap between **biology and morality**, confusing **impulse with inevitability**. The existence of a drive does not legitimize its expression, especially when it infringes on the dignity and autonomy of another person.

As we move forward, we must confront the central paradox: **how can a species with such profound cognitive abilities continue to excuse some of its darkest behaviours as though they were beyond its control?** How can a society that celebrates reason tolerate explanations for violence rooted in blind instinct?

The answers lie not in the brain alone, but in the **systems such as social, cultural, legal, that determine how we interpret and respond to those instincts.** In the next chapter, we will interrogate how patriarchal societies selectively weaponize biology to excuse male aggression, while simultaneously holding women responsible for provoking it. We will examine how the myth of the uncontrollable male libido persists due to its **usefulness** for maintaining power, preserving privilege, and avoiding accountability, despite its lack of truth,

PART II: THEORETICAL FOUNDATIONS

Chapter 6

The Hormonal Symphony of Puberty

In the more complex architecture of human sexuality, the act of sex is often explained as serving reproduction through straightforward biological imperative, in such a view, pleasure becomes an evolutionary footnote, a clever mechanism nature devised to ensure the continuation of the species. But **puberty**, that tumultuous gateway to sexual awakening, offers a far richer and more complicated story; the, one that reveals just how deeply the body and desire are intertwined, and how culture shapes, channels, and often distorts these impulses.

The **hormonal symphony of puberty** begins quietly but crescendos into a transformative upheaval, orchestrated largely by the dramatic rise of sex hormones. In boys, the **testosterone surge** triggers a cascade of changes: facial and body hair begins to grow, the voice deepens, muscles develop, and the penis matures, becoming capable of both erection and ejaculation. These outward signs are only the visible markers of a deeper inner transformation: the emergence of libido, the stirring of fantasies, the confusion of desire.,

In girls, **estrogen and progesterone** awaken the ovaries, initiating a parallel sequence of physiological change: the budding of breasts, the arrival of the first menstrual periods, the widening of hips, the softening of body contours, and the growth of pubic hair. These changes signify the capacity for reproduction and come with a surge in sexual curiosity and emotional intensity. If the male body becomes primed for penetration, the female body is simultaneously prepared to receive, to gestate, to nurture. These roles are inscribed by biology, but not without interpretation, not without the lens of culture, religion, and patriarchy bending biology into ideology.

Puberty becomes a **crucible of meaning** that extends far beyond biological transition, as hormones activate the machinery of reproduction, they also ignite a psychological and emotional reckoning. In the modern world, where reproduction is no longer the sole purpose of sex, the meaning of desire becomes murky. Pleasure, fantasy, shame, guilt, longing, all these elements become entangled in a storm of social expectation and internal contradiction.

Sexual desire during this phase extends far beyond reproduction. Indeed, the **pleasure of sex**, including the intense sensory rewards of touch, orgasm, and intimacy, emerges as a powerful force in its own right. It is no accident that the brain's **reward circuitry** lights up during sexual stimulation, as it does during the consumption of food or drugs. , From an evolutionary standpoint, pleasure ensures the continuation of the act; from a psychological perspective, it complicates everything.

The body's readiness for sex does not equate to emotional maturity. And yet, many societies have historically used puberty as a marker for **sexual availability**, particularly in girls. The moment the body signals reproductive potential, cultural narratives have swooped in to assign meaning: she is "ripe," she is "of age," she is "womanly." This biologically rooted transition has been exploited to justify **early marriage, sexual initiation,** even **abuse**, under the pretence that nature has already sanctioned her readiness.

In boys, the changes of puberty have often been interpreted as the unleashing of **uncontrollable urges**. The rise in testosterone is cited as evidence of an innate male sexual aggression, of boys "not being able to help themselves," of a libido so powerful it overwhelms rational thought. Here, biology becomes excuse, cloaked in the language of inevitability. But this, too, is a dangerous distortion. While testosterone is linked to increased sexual desire, it does not eliminate the capacity for **empathy, control**, or **consent.** Hormones may light the fire, but they do not dictate where, or how, it burns.

Moreover, the hormonal shifts of puberty occur across cultures, but the **meanings ascribed to them vary profoundly**. In some societies, puberty marks the beginning of sexual autonomy and exploration; in others, it signals the start of intense repression, modesty, and surveillance. This cultural variability reveals an essential truth: biology may initiate, but culture interprets. The same hormonal changes that flood a teenager with longing can be celebrated, feared, punished, or hidden, depending on where, and into what body, they emerge.

It is also during this time that youth encounter the first **societal**

scripts of gendered sexuality. Boys are taught that desire is natural and represents a sign of virility, while girls are warned to be cautious, modest, pure. The boy becomes the pursuer; the girl, the gatekeeper. These myths emerge from ideology while masquerading as natural facts, and when these gendered expectations collide with bodies suddenly thrumming with desire, the consequences can be profound.

The hormonal symphony of puberty is therefore more than just a biological process. It is the stage upon which **culture begins its most aggressive performance**, and often distorting the meaning of sex. While the body undergoes its ancient transformation, the mind is flooded not just with hormones, but with narratives: of masculinity, femininity, power, shame, and control.

If we are to understand **sexual violence** as a socially conditioned phenomenon rather than mere pathology or aberration, we must begin here, at puberty, where the animal and the human, the instinctual and the constructed, first collide. We must ask: **what are we teaching our children about entitlement? About whose desire matters? About who has the right to say yes or no?**

In the chapters to come, we will continue this investigation, moving beyond the hormonal and into the **moral and institutional frameworks** that allow certain expressions of desire to be valorized while others are punished. We will explore how sex becomes weaponized through systems of domination and how the innocence of a body's awakening gets twisted into a justification for its violation.

Clarifying the Myth: Testosterone and Aggression

The popular narrative that testosterone causes aggression is overly simplistic and scientifically misleading. While testosterone plays a role in **motivating competitive or status-seeking behaviour**, it does not inherently lead to violence. In fact, studies have shown that testosterone can **increase prosocial behaviour** when such behaviour is the path to gaining status or approval.

Historical examples further complicate the picture. **Eunuchs**, who were castrated before puberty and thus had extremely low testosterone levels, have held powerful and often militaristic roles in various empires, from the **Byzantine** and **Ottoman courts** to **imperial China**. Some were known for their **strategic ruthlessness**, political cunning, and even battlefield leadership. Their capacity for violence and authority challenges the idea that testosterone is a prerequisite for aggression or dominance.

Moreover, **context matters**. Social environment, cultural norms, and individual psychology all interact with biology. Testosterone may amplify certain tendencies, but it does not dictate behaviour. It is not a puppet master pulling the strings of violence.

Chapter 7

Bipedalism and the Shifting Landscape of Attraction

The journey from quadruped to biped represents not only a dramatic shift in how our ancestors moved through the world but also a profound transformation in how they were seen and how they saw each other. This evolutionary pivot, while initially motivated by the imperatives of survival, initiated a cascade of anatomical, neurological, and sexual changes that would redefine the terrain of human attraction.

As primate brains grew more advanced, our ancestors gained new flexibility in how they thought and responded to the world. They could remember more, plan ahead, and face dangers with sharper awareness. Life on the open savannas, where predators could hide in the tall grasses, made this vigilance especially important, and may have nudged evolution toward standing upright.

Walking on two legs was not an easy step. At first, it was less stable and slower than moving on four. But the advantages quickly added up: standing tall meant seeing farther, carrying tools or infants was easier, and hands were free for new kinds of work.

This change in posture unleashed a profound transformation. No longer bound to walking, the forelimbs became hands with unmatched dexterity: shaping tools, expressing emotions with subtle gestures, and even offering tenderness in touch.

But upright walking changed more than our reach; it reshaped our bodies, our sexuality, and even our sense of intimacy. In quadrupeds, the genitals are exposed at the rear, visible during mating. In humans, standing upright shifted them forward, nestling them between the thighs. This concealment altered how intimacy worked, bringing partners face to face and shifting sexual attention to new regions of the body.

One of the most striking of these regions is the breast. Unlike most mammals, where the chest swells only during nursing, human females develop permanent, rounded breasts at puberty. Their prominence has sparked long debate. Are they primarily about feeding, or do they also serve as signals of attraction? Their symmetry, visibility, and role in arousal suggest they carry layered meanings: biological, social, and erotic.

The breast, then, sits at a crossroads of biology and culture. It is a sign of fertility but also a site of fascination far beyond reproduction. Its placement, at the centre of the chest, in line with the gaze during face-to-face encounters makes it not only visible but symbolically powerful. In this sense, the move from rear-oriented sexuality to front-facing intimacy marked a deeper shift in human connection: from purely physical acts toward interactions rich with emotion, expression, and the gaze.

This shift also brought with it new forms of sexual signalling, along with opportunities for deception, desire, and conflict. Breasts, in this context, became more than biological organs. They became surfaces onto which societies projected sexuality, modesty, morality, and even shame. Their physical presence alone cannot explain their cultural weight. That burden comes from patriarchal systems that eroticize the female body while also policing it. What bipedalism initiated, civilization transformed, turning anatomy into symbol and the body into object.

The hidden position of the genitals also changed the erotic map of the body. The inner thighs, the curve of the hips, and the line of the back gained a new charge, not because of their biological function but because of their closeness to what was concealed. Concealment created curiosity. Curiosity grew into taboo, and taboo enabled control.

It is important to recognize that while evolutionary explanations can suggest why these anatomical changes occurred, they cannot explain the layers of meaning that cultures have added since. Breasts are not sexual by nature; they are made sexual by the societies that obsess over them. Likewise, the visibility or concealment of genitals does not, by itself, dictate shame, secrecy, or desire. These are cultural interpretations, shaped by history, gender, and power.

The story of bipedalism is therefore not only about walking upright. It is also about a new orientation of vision, touch, desire, and domination. When our ancestors stood, they did more than lift their heads. They exposed new surfaces, invited new gazes, and generated new meanings. The body stopped being only a tool for survival and became a stage for sexual symbolism, shaped first by biology and then rewritten by culture.

In the chapters ahead, we will continue to explore how these bodily shifts were absorbed into systems of control, such as those religious, legal, and psychological, that sought to govern not only who was allowed to desire but also who was allowed to be desired. We will look at how anatomy was treated as destiny, and how that supposed destiny was manipulated to serve power, often at the cost of consent, autonomy, and justice.

Chapter 8

The Body Awakens: Origins of Sexual Signalling

Puberty marks the shift from childhood to sexual maturity, a surge of hormones that reshapes both the body and the mind., The first stirrings of this transformation are often subtle: a budding breast, a deepening voice, the shadow of hair on once-smooth skin. Yet behind these physical signs lies a profound neurological and hormonal cascade, altering the terrain of identity, desire, and social interaction.

In girls, the development of breasts, called, **thelarche**, typically signals the beginning of this transition. Shortly thereafter, the ovaries accelerate the production of **estrogen** and **progesterone**, initiating the onset of menstruation, or **menarche**. The body's transformation includes a rapid growth spurt, the accumulation of subcutaneous fat around the hips and thighs, breast enlargement, and the widening of the pelvis, changes that evolution has linked to the body's preparation for potential childbearing. Alongside these changes emerge the psychological stirrings of desire, curiosity, and identity, all shaped by the intricate interplay of hormones, environment, and social messaging.

In boys, a parallel transformation unfolds. The **testes** begin producing large amounts of **testosterone**, the primary male sex hormone. This drives the growth of facial and body hair, deepens the voice, increases muscle mass, and contributes to the enlargement of the penis and scrotum. **Sperm production** begins, and with it comes the capacity, and the compulsion, for ejaculation. Erections become more frequent and often occur spontaneously, a reflection of both hormonal surges and psychological stimulation.

These changes are not merely mechanical. They mark the body's entry into a new domain of sexual meaning and social performance. Boys and girls begin to perceive each other, and themselves, through new lenses. Attraction takes shape, initially guided by instinct but increasingly modulated by cultural scripts about beauty, gender roles, and what it means to "be a man" or "be a woman."

Among humans, unlike most other animals, sexual signalling is not limited to visible genitals or scent-based cues. The **breast**, for instance, emerges as a uniquely human signal, both biologically and culturally charged. While animals in estrus emit pheromones to attract mates, human females possess no overt "heat" cycle. Instead, **secondary sexual characteristics**, like the rounded breast, become indirect signals of maturity and fertility. The human erotic economy is visual, psychological, and social. Attraction becomes decoupled from mere reproduction and aligned with pleasure, status, emotion, and meaning.

But this visual and symbolic economy is **asymmetric**. In many cultures, female breasts become both sexualized and regulated, fetishized by the male gaze and moralized by patriarchal norms. Unlike a bull indifferent to a cow's udder, human males are culturally conditioned to see the breast not only as a sign of motherhood but as a symbol of sexual desirability. This dual symbolism complicates the narrative of puberty, intertwining biology with societal expectations, shame, and power.

As puberty advances, both sexes seek outlets for their emerging desires. Some may explore their sexuality through solitary practices like **masturbation**, a natural and often necessary form of self-discovery. Others begin to navigate the treacherous terrain of intimacy and courtship. Here, too, evolutionary imperatives and social hierarchies intersect: the desire to attract, the competition for attention, and the subtle choreography of flirtation and consent.

Yet the process is far from uniform. Not all boys are driven by the same desires; not all girls develop in the same sequence. **Gender nonconforming adolescents, queer youth**, and those with atypical developmental trajectories often find themselves estranged from dominant narratives about puberty and attraction. For them, the journey into sexual maturity can be fraught with confusion, stigma, or silence.

To reduce puberty to a simple biological script, of boys chasing girls, and girls blooming into passive objects of attraction, is to miss its psychosocial richness and the ethical responsibility we bear in guiding young people through it. Sexual desire may be instinctual, but **respect, boundaries, and choice are learned**. As the body awakens, so too must the conscience

Chapter 9

The Body Awakens – Puberty, Desire

How adolescents come to understand and navigate these transformations is shaped as much by stories, customs, and society as by hormones. The biological changes of puberty set the stage, but it is the cultural narratives and social frameworks that give these changes meaning and direction

In most traditional societies, puberty was not met with confusion or silence, but with rituals that publicly acknowledged a child's entry into adulthood. Among the Maasai of Kenya, boys undergo circumcision rituals, symbolic of endurance and readiness. In parts of South India, girls who experience menarche are celebrated with elaborate functions, publicly marking their fertility. Though such customs vary widely in meaning and impact, they share a common goal: to make sense of a biological transformation through social narrative.

In contrast, modern urban societies often offer no such scripts, leaving adolescents to navigate their changing bodies in private, often with misinformation, shame, or fear.

Sexuality, when left unexplored or demonized, doesn't disappear, it simply goes underground, often reemerging in unhealthy or distorted ways. A boy who finds himself aroused by the sight of a girl may be met not with understanding, but with mockery or silence. A girl exploring her body may internalize guilt, thinking desire is something to be feared rather than understood. These early emotional experiences around sexuality can have lasting consequences: shaping confidence, inhibitions, and the capacity for intimacy in adult life.

Furthermore, pornography and media now play an outsized role in shaping adolescents' first exposure to sex. Unlike nature, which unfolds gradually, media delivers sex in stylized, distorted, and performative forms, often devoid of context, emotion, or ethics. This creates what psychologists call a "sexual script": a set of expectations about what sex is supposed to look like, how men and women should behave, who takes control, and who submits. These scripts can reinforce gender stereotypes, normalize aggression, and sideline the importance of consent and mutual pleasure.

Male adolescents, flooded with testosterone, often find themselves at the mercy of impulses they do not fully understand. Erections may arise spontaneously, triggered not by desire but by random stimuli or even stress. Wet dreams, nocturnal emissions, can surprise and confuse boys. Without guidance, such experiences may be wrongly perceived as shameful, rather than natural byproducts of a maturing reproductive system.

Female adolescents, meanwhile, are often socialized to see

themselves as the object of desire rather than its subject. They may begin to dress in ways that attract attention, but often without a clear understanding of why they do so, or whether the attention they receive is affirming or invasive. Some may find power in their emerging sexuality; others may experience it as vulnerability. The double bind is potent: be attractive, but not too inviting; be confident, but not promiscuous.

Crucially, both boys and girls must come to understand that desire is not a license. Sexual feelings are inevitable. Acting on them requires maturity, empathy, and consent. In evolutionary terms, desire may be a biological imperative, but in human society, it is mediated by culture, law, and ethics.

We are not slaves to our hormones. The prefrontal cortex, often called the "braking system" of the brain, matures more slowly than the limbic system that governs emotion and desire. This mismatch partly explains why teenagers often act impulsively: the systems that generate urges mature faster than the systems that regulate them. Recognizing this fact is not an excuse for transgression, but a call for guidance, education, and compassion. Adolescents must be taught not only what their bodies are doing, but how to steward these changes with integrity.

This chapter, then, is not just about biology. It is about agency, the capacity to understand and direct one's own bodily and emotional evolution. The breast is not merely a signal of sexual maturity. The erection is not merely a cue to act. These signs of change are the body's invitation to grow into selfhood, not just into the capacity to reproduce, but into the capacity to love, respect, and relate.

In many ways, puberty marks the awakening of a fundamental truth: that the body is not just a vessel for survival, but a site of pleasure, vulnerability, and connection. To enter adolescence is to begin writing the story of one's sexual self. And like all stories worth telling, it must be grounded in honesty, shaped by care, and guided by a vision that transcends mere instinct.

As the hormonal storm subsides and adulthood takes shape, the lessons of puberty linger: that desire is powerful, that the body is sacred, and that to seek intimacy is not merely to satisfy a drive, but to engage in one of the most profound acts of being human.

Chapter 10

The Enduring Drive – Sexuality, Vitality, and the Human Lifespan

Sex is one of the most fundamental aspects of human life, shaping not only our bodies but also our minds and societies. Its influence extends beyond biology, touching on the ways we relate to each other and make sense of ourselves in the world. Reducing sex to its hormonal consequences overlooks its fuller meaning in the human experience. Sex extends far beyond an instrument of reproduction or a longevity tonic driven by desire. It is a deeply emotional, social, and relational act, intertwined with how we understand love, connection, identity, and even mortality.

In long-term relationships, sexual intimacy can serve as a barometer of emotional closeness. Partners who maintain an active and consensual sexual life often report higher levels of bonding, communication, and overall satisfaction. This is not solely the domain of the young. Contrary to popular belief, sexual desire does not vanish with age. It may evolve, less impulsive, more emotionally nuanced, but the need for closeness, touch, and affirmation remains deeply human.

Indeed, older adults who continue to engage in sexual activity often report greater life satisfaction and fewer symptoms of depression. Regular sex in middle and later life has been linked to improved cardiovascular health, better sleep, enhanced immunity, and even neuroprotective effects, possibly delaying cognitive decline. These benefits are not merely a product of physical release, they stem from the intimacy, physical touch, and hormonal interplay that accompany meaningful sexual contact.

Yet, it would be naive to universalize this narrative. Gender plays a pivotal role in how aging and sexuality are experienced. For men, declining testosterone levels, sometimes termed andropause, can lead to reduced libido, erectile dysfunction, and mood fluctuations. For women, menopause marks a dramatic hormonal shift, bringing with it vaginal dryness, mood swings, and altered sexual responsiveness. These changes are biological, yes, but they are also laden with cultural meaning, often shaped by patriarchal ideas of desirability, youth, and female worth.

Society tends to erase the sexuality of older women, treating it as taboo or irrelevant, while older men's sexual lives are either glorified or pathologized. The availability of drugs like sildenafil (Viagra) reflects this asymmetry: while male sexual dysfunction is treated as a solvable problem, female sexual changes are often dismissed as psychological or inevitable. This reflects not just a biomedical gap but a cultural discomfort with aging, embodiment, and the idea that desire does not conform to a single life stage.

Moreover, queer and non-binary individuals often face even greater invisibility in conversations about sexuality and aging. Their needs, experiences, and identities are often overlooked, despite the fact that intimacy, love, and sexual fulfilment are universal aspirations, not privileges of youth or heterosexual norms.

We must also be cautious about medicalizing sexuality. The desire for sex should not become another benchmark of health, another metric of performance. Some people, due to personal, psychological, or asexual orientations, do not seek out sexual activity, and that too is valid. Health is defined by integrity, choice, and well-being in one's own body rather than by intercourse. Still, the message remains: a healthy sexual life, when desired and consensual, can be a powerful ally in the quest for longevity and fulfilment. It sustains hormonal balance while anchoring us to pleasure, to touch, to presence, and to the living moment. In the absence of fear, shame, or coercion, sex becomes a celebration of life itself

In this light, sexuality emerges as an enduring thread in the human fabric that extends beyond any fleeting stage Its meaning shifts over time, from procreation to passion, from identity to intimacy, but its capacity to nourish the body and soul remains constant.

As we age, our challenge is not to chase youth but to redefine vitality. Not as a number on a lab report or a fading standard of beauty, but as a capacity for connection, joy, and embodiment. In this way, sexuality, far from being a private or shameful subject, becomes a lifelong dialogue with desire, identity, and vitality, an affirmation that to feel, to touch, to be wanted, and to want, are among the most human of all instincts.

Let us then release sexuality from the prison of youth and procreation. Let us recognize it instead as an ever-evolving language, a conversation between body and spirit, hormones and emotion, longing and love, spoken across the arc of a lifetime.

Chapter 11

The Animalistic Urge vs. Human Complexity

Human sexuality is often described as a unique blend of biology and culture, instinct and interpretation. At its core lies a fundamental distinction: while animals' mate, humans have sex. This difference, though seemingly linguistic, reflects a profound divergence in evolutionary development and psychological experience. In the animal kingdom, mating is a biologically driven act, governed by cycles of fertility, pheromonal signalling, and dominance hierarchies. In contrast, human sexual behaviour is shaped not only by reproductive imperatives but also by emotional, social, and symbolic dimensions.

Among non-human animals, mating behaviour is typically straightforward. A female in estrus emits chemical cues that signal her readiness to reproduce. Males respond with ritualized displays, visual, auditory, or behavioural, that culminate in copulation. These interactions are efficient and largely devoid of ambiguity. Once fertilization occurs, the biological transaction is complete. In many species, the male's involvement ends immediately, and in some cases, his life does too.

Social animals such as primates and lions exhibit more complex mating systems, often structured around dominance hierarchies. Alpha males monopolize access to females, while subordinate males may attempt to mate through stealth or challenge. In species like chimpanzees and dolphins, mating involves social negotiation, alliances, and exchanges, yet the underlying goal remains the same: the propagation of genetic material.

Importantly, coercion in the animal world is not interpreted through a moral lens. A male forcibly mounting a female is considered a reproductive strategy, not a violation. Concepts such as consent, autonomy, and trauma do not apply in this context. The absence of psychological reflection or ethical judgment distinguishes animal mating from human sexual experience.

Human sexuality, however, evolved under markedly different conditions. One of the most significant adaptations in human evolution is the concealment of ovulation. Unlike many mammals, human females do not exhibit overt signs of fertility. This concealment altered the dynamics of pair bonding, encouraging males to remain close to their partners over extended periods. The result was a shift from episodic mating to sustained emotional and physical intimacy.

The human brain played a central role in this transformation. Neurochemicals such as oxytocin, dopamine, and serotonin began to link sexual pleasure with emotional closeness. Sex became not only a means of reproduction but also a mechanism for bonding, trust, and long-term partnership. Over time, human sexual behaviour expanded to include kissing, caressing, fantasizing, and other acts that serve no direct reproductive function. These behaviours reflect the increasing complexity of human desire and the symbolic nature of sexual expression.

"Sex in human society functions as a language, a system through which individuals communicate not only physical attraction but also vulnerability, power, insecurity, and affection Cultural narratives, religious doctrines, and literary traditions have long used sexual imagery to explore themes of divinity, identity, and transcendence. Unlike animals, humans may seek sex for reasons unrelated to reproduction, and conversely, may avoid it despite biological readiness.

This duality presents a central paradox: humans are animals governed by instinct, yet they interpret those instincts through the lens of culture. The physiological markers of desire, such as increased heart rate, pupil dilation, and hormonal surges, remain deeply embedded in our biology. However, these impulses are regulated by social norms, legal frameworks, and ethical considerations. Human societies demand that sexual behaviour conform to standards of consent, reciprocity, and morality. When these standards are violated, the response is not merely biological but deeply moral and psychological.

Despite these layers of regulation, the animalistic aspects of human sexuality persist. The immediacy of attraction, the urge to dominate or submit, and the fetishization of specific body parts are remnants of our evolutionary past. Modern phenomena such as pornography, romantic fantasy, and even sexual violence reflect the ongoing tension between primal drives and cultural constraints. The animal within us is not eradicated, it is reframed, reinterpreted, and often disguised by the conventions of civilization.

Understanding this tension requires a balanced perspective. Reducing sex to mere biology ignores its emotional and symbolic richness. Conversely, viewing it as entirely transcendent overlooks the instinctual forces that continue to shape human behaviour. Humans occupy a unique space between beast and angel, capable of profound empathy and abstract thought, yet still subject to the raw impulses of desire.

Sex, therefore, represents an evolving dialogue between the body and the mind, between instinct and meaning. It functions as a mirror in which the animal and the human gaze at one another, rarely in perfect harmony, yet always in conversation. To engage in sexual intimacy is to participate in this dialogue. To study it is to listen closely to what it reveals about who we are, where we come from, and what we seek, not only in others, but in ourselves

Chapter 12

The Dual Evolution of Breasts

The human body is an archive, a living manuscript of evolution, where each fold, curve, and gland whispers stories of adaptation, survival, and desire. Among its most enigmatic and symbolically charged features is the human breast. At once a biological instrument of nourishment and an object of seduction, the breast occupies a dual realm: functional and symbolic, maternal and erotic, mammalian and mythic. In no other species are mammary glands as conspicuous, as permanent, or as culturally saturated as they are in *Homo sapiens*.

In the broader mammalian order, the function of breasts is straightforward. Milk-producing glands appear along ventral lines, often in multiples, to accommodate large litters. These glands swell temporarily during pregnancy and lactation, then recede into biological anonymity. Their purpose is singular: to feed.

Humans, however, diverged from this pattern. Our species evolved only two breasts, situated high on the chest, and, perhaps more strikingly, they develop fully during puberty, not pregnancy. This anticipatory swelling, long before any child requires nourishment, suggests a new evolutionary function: not sustenance, but signal.

This is the paradox of the human breast: it advertises before it performs, seduces before it nourishes very presence, rounded, protruding, firm, serves as a perpetual emblem of reproductive fitness beyond immediate maternal care, sculpted by millennia of sexual selection. Unlike the cyclical swellings of estrus seen in our primate cousins, the human breast broadcasts availability continuously, blurring the line between fertility and foreplay, biology and semiotics.

What, then, are these breasts saying?

Evolutionary psychologists suggest they form part of a broader reproductive display complex. Alongside the waist-to-hip ratio of approximately 0.7, the distribution of gluteofemoral fat, the softness of skin, and the curvature of the spine, the breast becomes a visual shorthand, an embodied résumé of fertility, youth, and vitality. Interestingly, the fatty composition of the breast is not functionally tied to lactation. It exists, in part, to be seen, to attract, to allure.

Male attraction to breasts follows a near-universal logic. Across cultures, and even among prepubescent boys, preferences emerge for specific shapes, sizes, and proportions. These desires often precede cultural indoctrination, suggesting a biological core, a neural circuitry shaped by ancestral environments where certain visual cues correlated with higher chances of reproductive success. The breast, then, functions as both body part and evolutionary language, decoded instinctively by the visual cortex and interpreted through the shifting grammar of culture.

Yet this biological determinism is insufficient to explain the full erotic charge of the breast. For humans, sex is not merely sensory, it is semiotic. Our desires are interpreted, not just felt. A breast can be a source of life, a subject of shame, a symbol of freedom, an object of fetish, or a battleground of politics, depending on where, when, and how it is seen. In some cultures, it is taboo to expose; in others, to conceal. In advertising, it sells; in religion, it tempts; in art, it reveals the sacred and the profane.

This symbolic layering has rendered the breast an object of perpetual tension. What remains unsaid is what the breast has come to mean beyond biology: the implicit social codes it carries, the histories it evokes, the ambivalence it inspires. A woman may feel both empowered and objectified, liberated and scrutinized, depending on the gaze cast upon her chest, and behind that gaze, whether appreciative, judgmental, or fetishizing, lies an ancient circuitry wired to survival, now tangled in postmodern complexity.

The same breast that feeds the newborn is photoshopped for billboards. The same organ that evokes comfort and safety is weaponized in moral panics and censorship debates. Even medical discourses, breast cancer awareness, reconstructive surgery, hormonal therapies, reveal the deep cultural stakes encoded in this body part. A mastectomy does not merely remove tissue; it reshapes identity. An augmentation is not just aesthetic; it is aspirational, sometimes existential.

Thus, the breast becomes both body part and cultural canvas. It tells us who we are, what we value, what we fear, and what we long for It holds maternal tenderness and erotic provocation in a single silhouette. It is where the child's latching and the lover's gaze converge, two forms of intimacy, rooted in vastly different timelines of evolution, yet meeting on the same flesh.

What remains unsaid is this: that biology is never destiny. The human breast may have evolved as an honest signal of reproductive health, but what it means, what it signifies, evokes, or conceals, is shaped by language, memory, and power. We do not simply see breasts; we read them. And like all texts, they are open to interpretation, revision, erasure, and resistance.

The breast becomes a powerful metaphor for human sexuality itself; rooted in the body yet shaped by the mind. It carries a dual inheritance of nature and culture, blending hunger with desire, nourishment with longing. To understand the breast is to confront the very essence of what makes us human: the ability to transform instinct into symbolism, function into ritual, and flesh into story.

Chapter 13

Sexual Choices and Differences

Human sexuality forms a textured terrain shaped by biological asymmetries, psychological architectures, and cultural scripts rather than a flat plane of uniform desire. Though men and women belong to the same species, their sexual psychologies reflect evolutionary pressures that have left enduring imprints on behaviour, preference, and intimacy. Yet even as we explore these differences, we must tread with care. Description differs from justification, and explanation differs from excuse.

At the biological level, the sexual act is asymmetrical by design. The male orgasm is direct and projective: the culmination of arousal results in the ejaculation of semen, a single moment that delivers the potential for fertilization. The female orgasm, however, is more complex and less predictable. During orgasm, the rhythmic muscular contractions of the vaginal and pelvic walls create a suction effect, drawing sperm inward toward the cervix and fallopian tubes, thereby increasing the chances of conception. Vaginal secretions, stimulated by arousal, provide lubrication that transforms the act from painful to pleasurable, another evolved feature that supports reproductive success.

Crucially, while male orgasm is almost always tied to ejaculation, female orgasm is not a reproductive necessity. This evolutionary puzzle has invited wide-ranging hypotheses, from the "byproduct theory" (female orgasm as a developmental echo of male physiology) to the pair-bonding theory, which sees female pleasure as an incentive for long-term partnership and selective mating.

Unlike most non-human species, human females experience concealed ovulation, which decouples sexual receptivity from reproductive timing. This means sexual desire and intimacy are not confined to fertility windows but are spread across the menstrual cycle, and across the lifespan. The result is an intricate emotional, hormonal, and psychological system in which sexuality becomes not just about procreation but about connection, status, affection, and identity.

The asymmetry of reproductive investment deepens this divide. A single fertile male, in theory, can impregnate hundreds of women in a year. A fertile woman, however, can produce at most one child per year, sometimes fewer. The evolutionary consequences of this are significant. Natural selection has shaped women to be more selective in their sexual choices, often prioritizing long-term traits like resource provision, stability, and commitment. Men, by contrast, have evolved to pursue both short-term mating opportunities and long-term bonds, depending on environmental and social conditions.

This does not mean that men are inherently promiscuous or that women are naturally monogamous. It means that on average, their strategies reflect the differential costs of reproduction. Human behaviour is plastic, and culture can either amplify or dampen these evolutionary inclinations.

Yet when these biological patterns are interpreted simplistically, they can become dangerous, especially when used to rationalize sexual coercion or violence. For example, some evolutionary psychologists have suggested that men's stronger baseline sex drive or preference for sexual variety might partially explain the prevalence of male-perpetrated rape. But this line of thinking flirts dangerously with biological determinism, confusing explanation with exoneration. Rape is not sex, it is violence. It is an abuse of power, not a misfiring of desire. No evolutionary theory can justify the violation of another's autonomy.

Similarly, psychoanalytic theories have historically painted a troubling picture of female sexuality. Early Freudian models proposed that women were inherently narcissistic, masochistic, and passive, and some theorists even suggested that women unconsciously "wanted" to be dominated or raped, a notion that has been rightly condemned as both pseudoscientific and misogynistic. The concept of the 'professional victim,' with an alleged inner need to be violated, dehumanizes survivors while pathologizing trauma itself. No one ever 'invites' a crime. No one is biologically programmed to suffer.

Such distortions reveal the dangers of reading biological sex differences through the lens of patriarchal power. They collapse the richness of female desire into a caricature, and they reduce male sexuality to a brutish impulse devoid of ethics or emotional nuance. Both are impoverished views of human intimacy.

It is more accurate, and more just, to say that men and women are shaped by different pressures, and that these have influenced their sexual psychologies in different ways. Women may, on average, be more attuned to emotional connection, relational context, and long-term partner quality. Men may be, on average, more visually stimulated, more prone to short-term desire, and more sensitive to novelty. These are statistical tendencies that differ from fixed destinies Individuals vary widely, and socialization plays an enormous role in shaping behaviour.

The cyclical nature of female libido, affected by pregnancy, menstruation, nursing, and menopause, contrasts with the relatively steady baseline of male sexual drive. But even here, variance is key. Some women experience heightened desire during pregnancy; some men lose interest in sex under stress. Libido becomes a dance between hormones, context, and culture rather than fate

Cognitive sex differences, too, have been observed: women often outperform men in verbal fluency and emotional recognition; men tend to excel in spatial navigation. These differences may reflect evolutionary adaptations, female ancestors needing to read social cues in cooperative groups, males needing to hunt or defend territory. But like all such findings, they exist on a spectrum and overlap far more than they diverge.

In the end, sexual differences between men and women represent evidence of evolutionary trade-offs rather than a battleground of superiority or blame. They are shaped by millions of years of reproductive strategy, layered with culture, morality, and meaning. We must understand these differences to foster empathy, dialogue, and mutual respect while avoiding essentialization or division

The challenge lies in balancing biological reality with ethical responsibility. We cannot unmake the past that shaped our bodies, but we can choose how we live in them, how we understand each other, how we love, how we respect boundaries, and how we imagine a future where sexual difference is a source not of conflict, but of complexity.

Chapter 14

Rethinking Perversion

Human sexuality is a complex tapestry, woven from threads of biology, emotion, imagination, and cultural conditioning. Across history, it has been policed, pathologized, repressed, and celebrated, sometimes simultaneously. To grasp its intricacies, we turn to frameworks that attempt to decode desire: from early psychoanalytic theories to contemporary clinical diagnostics. Yet, in doing so, we must ask: Who defines the normal? Who defines the deviant? And what power structures lie beneath those definitions?

Freud's ideas shaped much of how we think about sexual development. He believed that early childhood is a key time when our sexual identity and deep desires take shape. According to Freud, boys go through the "Oedipus complex," feeling unconscious attraction toward their mothers and rivalry with their fathers, eventually resolving this by identifying with their fathers and adopting social rules and gender roles. Later, Jung described a similar idea for girls called the "Electra complex," where the father becomes the desired figure and the mother a rival. Freud's views about girls were less clear and often problematic, implying that female development was incomplete or conflicted. These early ideas reveal the limits of old-fashioned psychoanalysis.

Today, psychologists see sexuality as much more fluid and shaped by culture, relationships, personal history, and individual choice. Desire no longer follows a single path but spreads across a wide spectrum influenced by gender, orientation, trauma, and agency.

The word "perversion" was once a catch-all label for any sexual interest that didn't fit strict, socially approved norms. These norms, set by religion, law, and culture, favoured heterosexual, monogamous, and reproductive sex. Behaviours like voyeurism, exhibitionism, sadism, and masochism were thrown together as "perversions," without considering consent or harm. This label was moralistic and often harmful because it blurred the important difference between sexual diversity and abuse. It failed to separate voluntary, harmless activities from those that violate others.

Modern psychology prefers the term "paraphilia" to describe unusual or intense sexual interests outside typical scenarios. But having a paraphilic interest isn't a disorder by itself. Problems arise only when these interests cause distress, harm daily life, or involve non-consenting people. Understanding this distinction is crucial. For example, adult BDSM practiced consensually can be healthy, while voyeurism without consent is a serious violation. This shift from "perversion" to "paraphilia" marks a move from moral judgment to thoughtful clinical understanding cantered on consent, harm, and respect.

Even this modern approach must be seen in context. Who

defines what counts as distress? How do culture and bias shape our ideas about mental health? Which behaviours get punished, and why? Such questions become urgent when we confront sexual violence. Rape, often wrongly described alongside sexual "deviances," is not about unusual desire. It is about power and control, the violation of consent, and the objectification of bodies. Recognizing rape as a social and political problem, beyond a mere medical one is vital. It's a tool used within systems like patriarchy, war, caste, and racism to dominate others. To label rape as a mental illness misses the bigger picture. Instead, we need to challenge and change the systems that allow it to happen.

Some animals show the Bruce effect, where the presence of a new male can cause females to lose pregnancies. While interesting, this biological behaviour doesn't straightforwardly apply to humans. Cases where women harm children following new relationships stem more from psychological pain, social pressures, or illness. Still, the Bruce effect reminds us that reproduction and relationships are deeply tied to context. Our behaviours are influenced by both biology and the social world we live in.

Chapter 15

The Shadow of the Mind, Violence Through the Lens of Severe Psychiatric Disorder,

The preceding chapters have explored various facets of human behaviour, delving into the complexities of social interactions, cognitive processes, and emotional landscapes. Yet there exists a darker territory, a realm where the intricate machinery of the mind malfunctions in profound ways, sometimes manifesting in acts of violence that defy comprehension. This chapter ventures into that unsettling domain, examining instances of extreme violence through the lens of severe psychiatric disorders. The cases discussed are not merely accounts of criminal acts; they serve as stark reminders of the devastating consequences when profound mental illness intertwines with the capacity for inflicting harm.

Consider the harrowing case of Shanbhuag. The perpetrator's simultaneous acts of sexual assault and strangulation point toward a confluence of disturbed motivations. The act of strangulation, beyond its immediate physical violence, suggests a desire for dominance and control intertwined with sexual violation. This dual abuse hints at a deeply fractured psyche, where sexual gratification is pathologically linked with aggression and a disregard for human life.

The Nirbhaya case presents an even more chilling tableau of brutality. The sheer sadism displayed, particularly by the juvenile offender, with the piercing of the victim's body and the accompanying taunts, speaks to a profound lack of empathy and the presence of intense, destructive urges. That such cruelty emanated from a young individual, exposed to a harsh environment and the company of adult offenders, underscores the potential for environmental factors to exacerbate underlying vulnerabilities or contribute to the development of severely antisocial and violent tendencies. This case compels us to consider the complex interplay between individual psychology and social context in the genesis of extreme violence.

Moving further into the abyss of human depravity, the examples of necrophiliacs like Umesh Reddy and the Dandupalya gang illustrate the horrifying extremes of paraphilic disorders and a complete erosion of societal norms. The act of engaging sexually with dying or deceased individuals, irrespective of gender, signifies a radical departure from normative human behaviour and points toward severe disturbances in sexual arousal patterns, object relations, and moral compass. The group dynamic of the Dandupalya gang, including the involvement of women and elderly members, further highlights the potential for shared psychopathology to amplify and normalize the most abhorrent behaviours within a closed social system.

The Nithari killings introduce another layer of psychological disturbance: that of the seemingly innocuous predator. The perpetrators' ability to blend into everyday life, masquerading as ordinary individuals, underscores the deceptive nature of some severe mental illnesses. Their capacity for prolonged and calculated acts of violence, coupled with the alleged consumption of their victims' remains, suggests a descent into a psychotic realm far removed from reality and marked by extreme deviance. The neighbours' unsuspecting observations of the perpetrators' seemingly normal behaviour after the murders serve as a chilling reminder of how effectively severe psychopathology can be masked.

Historically, groups like the Thuggee and the Phansigars demonstrated highly organized and ruthless methods of violence. The Phansigars' "science of finishing off their victims" to expedite decomposition reveals a cold, calculated approach to murder, prioritizing the elimination of evidence. While the specific psychiatric underpinnings of these historical groups may be difficult to ascertain retrospectively, their systematic brutality and disregard for human life suggest the presence of severely disordered thought processes and a capacity for extreme violence, potentially amplified by group dynamics and cultural norms of the time. The comparison to contemporary killers suggests that while the manifestations of violence may evolve, the underlying potential for extreme human cruelty, possibly rooted in severe psychological disturbance, persists.

The case of Dominique Pelicot, who allegedly drugged his wife and facilitated her abuse by numerous men, highlights the potential for one individual's pathology to inflict widespread harm. His testimony, citing traumatic childhood experiences and the influence of online interactions, suggests a complex interplay of personal history and external triggers in the development of his deviant behaviour. The act of filming the abuses further points to a significant disturbance in his sexual functioning and a profound violation of trust and intimacy.

The horrific Fritzl case provides a disturbing illustration of long-term captivity, incestuous rape, and the devastating impact of severe personality disorders. Josef Fritzl's history of suspected rapes and murders, coupled with his own account of a traumatic childhood and a self-proclaimed innate "evil side," underscores the potential for early life experiences and inherent psychological vulnerabilities to culminate in extreme acts of violence and control. The diagnosis of a severe combined personality disorder with borderline, schizotypal, and schizoid features, along with a sexual disorder, offers a clinical framework for understanding the profound disturbances in his personality and behaviour. His premeditated plan to imprison his daughter to indulge his "evil side" reveals a chilling level of self-awareness regarding his pathological urges and a complete lack of remorse.

Collectively, these cases underscore the critical link between severe psychiatric disorders and the capacity for extreme violence. They highlight the diverse ways in which such disorders can manifest, ranging from impulsive acts of brutality to meticulously planned and prolonged campaigns of abuse. Furthermore, the potential for individuals with similar severe psychiatric disorders to coalesce and amplify their destructive tendencies, as seen in some of the gang-related cases, presents a significant societal threat.

The observation that hidden psychos may exist within

communities, sometimes with their disturbing behaviours known but unreported, points to a critical failure in societal awareness and intervention. The ubiquity of mental health issues, coupled with the potential for even seemingly "normal" individuals to harbour dangerous psychologies, necessitates a shift in how we understand and address these problems.

The argument for treating this issue as a public health concern is compelling. Relying solely on the legal and enforcement systems, which typically intervene after a crime has been committed, is insufficient. A proactive approach that prioritizes early identification, comprehensive psychiatric intervention, and destigmatization of mental health issues is crucial. This requires a multi-faceted strategy involving increased access to mental healthcare, public awareness campaigns to encourage reporting of concerning behaviours, and the development of effective risk assessment and management tools.

The cases presented in this chapter serve as grim reminders of the devastating intersection of severe psychiatric disorder and extreme violence. Understanding the psychological underpinnings of such acts is not about excusing them, but rather about gaining critical insights that can inform more effective prevention and intervention strategies. By recognizing this as a significant public health challenge, society can move towards a more proactive and compassionate approach to mitigating the risks associated with severe mental illness and fostering safer communities for all

Chapter 16

Rape as Social Disease

Rape is often viewed through the narrow lens of criminality, a violent act that demands legal consequence. While this framing is essential for justice, it is also limiting. It focuses on the immediate violation while overlooking the deeper currents that sustain and spread this form of violence across societies and generations. What if we shifted our perspective, not to excuse or downplay the act, but to better understand and dismantle the systems that enable it?

This chapter proposes a radical reframing: to view rape as both crime and social disease, a pathology where the sickness resides in one person or system, and the suffering in another. Like a disease, rape often incubates silently in environments of denial, stigma, and power imbalance before it erupts into individual acts of violence. And like any epidemic, it thrives where institutions fail, where silence festers, and where cultural immunity is weak.

From this public health vantage point, rape can be understood as a multi-factorial phenomenon, one that demands the tools of epidemiology, mental health, education, and social transformation. It is not enough to prosecute the act; we must also diagnose the conditions, treat the trauma, and immunize society against its recurrence.

Rape, in this model, functions as an individual crime while serving as a symptom of a larger societal dysfunction It spreads through cultural norms, structural inequalities, and systemic silences. To treat it only at the level of law enforcement is like applying a bandage to a deep infection. We must examine the conditions that allow this violence to persist and replicate.

This reframing also invites us to consider how trauma, power, and social conditioning interact in ways that make rape a personal violation while constituting a public health crisis It is a form of violence that disproportionately affects women and marginalized communities, yet its roots lie in the very structures that shape our collective lives, patriarchy, caste, racism, militarism, and economic inequality.

In this light, prevention becomes more than just self-defence classes or harsher sentencing. It becomes a matter of education, cultural change, and institutional accountability. It means teaching consent as a fundamental value, not a legal technicality. It means dismantling the myths that normalize coercion and silence survivors. It means recognizing that rape emerges from what the norm has allowed instead of deviating from it.

Calling rape, a disease means acknowledging its systemic nature while avoiding traditional medicalization, its ability to spread, to mutate, and to embed itself in the fabric of society. And like any disease, it requires a collective response combining punishment with prevention; treatment with transformation

Chapter 17

Understanding Epidemiology

Epidemiology is the cornerstone of public health, a discipline that helps us understand how diseases emerge, spread, and can be controlled. While often associated with outbreaks and pandemics, epidemiology is much broader in scope. It is the science of patterns, causes, and effects of health and disease conditions in defined populations. In essence, epidemiology is the study of health in society.

An epidemic is a sudden rise in the number of cases of a disease beyond what is normally expected in a particular population or area. It represents a disruption, an unexpected surge that requires immediate attention and action. Epidemics can be confined to a single community or spread widely across regions and countries, sometimes evolving into pandemics, like COVID-19. History offers many examples of epidemics, including the Black Death in the Middle Ages, cholera outbreaks in the 19th century, influenza pandemics in the 20th century, and more recent outbreaks such as SARS, MERS, Ebola, Nipah virus, and COVID-19.

The Epidemiological Triad

Epidemiology is the scientific study of how diseases affect populations. It investigates the distribution (who, when, where) and determinants (why, how) of health-related events. Epidemiologists are the detectives of public health, they trace outbreaks, identify risk factors, and recommend interventions to prevent future cases.

Simply put, Epidemiology is the study of the patterns, causes, and effects of health and disease conditions in populations.

To understand how diseases spread, epidemiologists use a model called the epidemiological triad, which consists of three components:

1. Agent – The cause of the disease (e.g., virus, bacteria, parasite).
2. Host – The organism (usually human) that can be infected.
3. Environment – External factors that affect the agent and the host, such as climate, sanitation, and social conditions.

This triad helps identify points of intervention. For example, in the case of dengue fever:

- The agent is the dengue virus.
- The hosts are both humans and mosquitoes.
- The environment includes stagnant water, poor drainage, and crowded urban areas that allow mosquitoes to thrive.

Epidemiology, though closely linked with infectious diseases, extends far beyond them. Its tools and methods are also used to study chronic illnesses like diabetes and heart disease, mental health conditions, environmental risks, injury prevention, and the social factors that influence health. This broad application makes epidemiology essential for understanding and improving overall public health.

By empowering individuals and communities to interpret public health warnings, take informed precautions during outbreaks, support prevention efforts, advocate for policy changes, and recognize patterns of harm beyond biology such as violence, inequality, and trauma, epidemiology provides vital tools. In a world shaped by globalization, climate change, and social challenges, it offers not only means for survival but also pathways toward justice.

PART III: COMPREHENSIVE PROBLEM ANALYSIS

Chapter 18

The Rapedemiological Tetrad:

While the legal definition of rape focuses on the act of violation itself, understanding why and how it occurs requires a broader analytical framework. Drawing inspiration from epidemiology: the study of patterns, causes, and effects of health and disease in populations, we introduce the Rapedemiological Tetrad, a public health model that breaks sexual violence into four interconnected components, much like how epidemiologists track infectious disease outbreaks.

1. Victim Vulnerability (Host Susceptibility)
2. Perpetrator Agency (Pathogenic Factor)
3. Facilitating Environment (Transmission Vector)
4. Influential Factors (Epidemiological Determinants)

By dissecting each of these elements, we can gain a more comprehensive understanding of the complex dynamics that contribute to this pervasive societal issue, moving beyond simplistic blame and towards more nuanced and effective prevention strategies.

1. Victim Vulnerability: Situational Risk, Not Inherent Fault

It is paramount to establish that the ultimate responsibility for the act of rape rests solely and unequivocally with the perpetrator. Any analysis of victim characteristics or circumstances must be approached with extreme caution to avoid perpetuating victim-blaming narratives. Instead, the concept of "victim vulnerability" within this tetrad focuses on identifying situational factors that may increase an individual's risk of encountering a perpetrator in a conducive environment. Examining historical cases, not to assign blame but to understand the dynamics of risk, can be instructive:

- **The Case of Aruna Shanbaug:** Aruna Shanbaug was a nurse working in a Mumbai hospital. One evening, while on duty, she was brutally attacked and raped by a ward boy. What made her particularly vulnerable was her position within the institution – she was working late, in a setting where a power imbalance existed between staff members. Her reliance on the hospital environment for her safety and livelihood was tragically exploited. The verbal exchange she had with the attacker prior to the assault, while in no way excusing his actions, highlights how even everyday interactions can turn deadly when a predator with malicious intent has access to someone in a dependent position. Aruna's subsequent decades spent in a vegetative state serve as a harrowing testament to the catastrophic consequences of such institutional vulnerability.

- **The Shakti Oil Mill Incident:** A young woman in Delhi was returning home when she was abducted and taken to an abandoned oil mill. This location, isolated and far from public view, presented a facilitating environment for the perpetrators. The woman's vulnerability was heightened by her presence in an unfamiliar and deserted place, where the risk of being seen or helped was minimal. Her decision to enter this space, perhaps out of necessity or a momentary lapse in awareness of the potential danger, tragically placed her in a situation where the perpetrators could act with little fear of immediate intervention. This case starkly illustrates how the physical environment can create zones of increased risk for individuals.

- **The Nirbhaya Tragedy:** Jyoti Singh Pandey, known as Nirbhaya, boarded a private bus in Delhi with a male friend. In a seemingly ordinary act of using public transportation, she placed her trust in the system and the other passengers. However, this trust was brutally betrayed by a group of men on the bus who subjected her to a horrific gang rape and assault. Nirbhaya's vulnerability stemmed from the inherent uncertainties of public spaces, where one is in close proximity to strangers whose intentions are unknown. Her case underscores the tragic reality that even within shared, everyday environments, the potential for extreme violence exists, and the reliance on the assumed safety of public spaces can have devastating consequences when predatory individuals are present. The lack of intervention from other passengers further highlights how a breakdown in social responsibility can exacerbate vulnerability.

- In additional cases, such as the Hyderabad veterinarian who was lured to an isolated parking area and subjected to prolonged, agonizing violence, the secluded location and absence of surveillance made her tragically vulnerable. Similarly, a young doctor at RG Kar Hospital became a target after being perceived as a threat; the easy accessibility of her room and the perpetrator's addiction to violent pornography contributed to the brutal attack.

These examples are not presented to suggest fault but to highlight how a confluence of factors, a potential victim, a motivated perpetrator, and a conducive environment, can tragically align.

It is crucial to reiterate that these examples are not presented as "mistakes" on the part of the women that in any way justify the assaults they endured. Instead, they serve as stark illustrations of situations where a confluence of factors: the presence of a potential victim, the intent of a perpetrator, and an environment conducive to the crime are tragically aligned. Furthermore, even in environments perceived as safe, the potential for sudden and brutal violence can erupt. The very buses carrying Nirbhaya or the spaces occupied by groups of individuals can harbour predators, and those who might be expected to intervene can instead become complicit. This unsettling reality underscores the limitations of relying solely on intuition or a perceived sense of security. A heightened awareness of potential risks, while psychologically burdensome, may be a necessary adaptation in a society grappling with such pervasive violence.

he reality of sexual assault reveals a troubling pattern of vulnerability affecting people from all walks of life. These stories are not about blaming victims but highlight how offenders take advantage of weaknesses, dependencies, and social pressures. Whether in a sterile hospital room or what should be the safety of one's home, danger often arises where power is unbalanced and isolation occurs. Think of those most helpless among us: patients on ventilators or elderly people in care homes, whose survival depends on others, creating a dangerous imbalance that some may exploit. Likewise, vulnerable individuals living in orphanages or shelters are at risk, as are domestic workers who may suffer abuse but remain silent for fear of losing their jobs.

The innocence of childhood and the earnest desires of youth can also be twisted into tools of manipulation. A child lured by the simple promise of chocolate, a student burdened by the anxiety of academic failure and the tempting offer of illicit aid, these scenarios highlight how basic needs and aspirations can be insidiously exploited. The human longing for connection, for love and security, can likewise be perverted, as seen in instances where the promise of marriage becomes a deceptive lure into harm's way.

Physical and mental limitations further widen the chasm of vulnerability. Individuals with physical disabilities or intellectual impairments may face heightened risks due to their reliance on others and a potentially reduced capacity to understand, resist, or articulate the abuse they endure. The very real fear of societal stigma, the dread of being labelled a "victim," can be so powerful that it silences those who have experienced attempted rape, trapping them in a prison of fear and isolation.

The idea of family as a safe and sacred space can be shattered in the most brutal ways, often driven by strict social rules and a need for control. One tragic example is the story of a village girl who eloped with someone from a different caste, hoping to break free from societal limits. When she returned home, instead of understanding, she was subjected to a horrific betrayal by her own brother and father. This terrible act shows how deeply social hierarchies and shame can be used as weapons, turning family members into abusers and making the home a place of horror.

Even moments meant for happiness and celebration can be ruined. Consider the bride who was attacked by her cousin alone in her dressing room just before her wedding. On what should have been the happiest day of her life, surrounded by music and guests, she was vulnerable in a quiet, private moment. The perpetrator, someone who knew where she was, struck during that brief pause in the celebration. The joy outside contrasted sharply with the fear she felt inside. Her silence afterward, driven by the fear of shaming her family and destroying her marriage, reveals how social pressures often keep victims quiet and perpetrators free.

The chilling account of the woman brutalized by her husband's brother, forced to live in the same house as her attacker, underscores the profound helplessness and isolation that many survivors face. Trapped within a hostile environment, with no apparent avenue for escape or justice, their trauma is compounded by the constant presence of their abuser. These narratives, though distinct in their details, converge on a central, disturbing truth: vulnerability to sexual assault is not confined to specific demographics or circumstances. It is a shadow that can fall across any life, exploited by those who seek to exert power and inflict harm. Understanding these diverse pathways to vulnerability is not about assigning blame but about illuminating the insidious nature of this crime and the urgent need for a society that actively works to dismantle the structures and attitudes that allow such violations to occur. Both women share their stories anonymously in a women's magazine to seek psychological counselling.

2. Perpetrator Agency: The Intent and Capacity for Harm

The second critical element of the Rapedemiological tetrad is the perpetrator, the active agent who commits the act of sexual violence. Understanding the characteristics, motivations, and capacities of these individuals is paramount for developing effective prevention and intervention strategies. Research across various disciplines has yielded a complex and often disturbing picture of the perpetrators of rape:

- **Ubiquity of Perpetrators:** The sad truth is that people who commit rape come from all walks of life. They aren't just the scary strangers in the dark alleys we sometimes imagine. They can be people we know and even trust – family members like brothers, sons, and fathers; people in positions of authority like teachers or religious leaders; friends we thought were safe; or yes, even complete strangers we meet in everyday life. When someone we trust abuses that trust, especially in families or when they have power over us, it can cause incredibly deep and lasting emotional damage.

- **Intergenerational and Collective Perpetration:**

There are horrifying stories of abuse that happens across generations in families, like grandparents abusing grandchildren. There are also cases where multiple people in a family commit these acts together. These terrible situations show how deeply rooted power imbalances can be and how sexual violence can become something that's seen as normal within certain groups. These extreme examples make it clear that we urgently need to tackle these deep-seated problems in our society and challenge the harmful ideas that allow them to happen.

The motivations behind rape are multifaceted and complex, ranging from expressions of power and control to the acting out of distorted sexual fantasies and the manifestation of underlying psychological disorders.

3. Facilitating Environment: The Context for Commission

The "environment" within this framework encompasses any physical or social context that provides the opportunity and conditions for a perpetrator to commit rape. This extends beyond mere geographical location to include social norms, power dynamics, and the absence of protective factors:

- **Physical Spaces of Vulnerability:** As illustrated by the Shakti Oil Mill case, isolated or unsupervised physical locations can create opportunities for perpetrators. However, the environment can be far more insidious, as demonstrated by the wedding chamber scenario, where a seemingly safe and intimate space became the site of a devastating assault due to the perpetrator's access and the victim's vulnerability within that context.

- **Institutional and Authority-Based Environments:** Schools, religious institutions, and other settings where individuals hold positions of power over others can become environments conducive to abuse. The inherent power imbalance can be exploited by perpetrators to coerce and control victims, often with a reduced risk of detection or intervention due to fear of reprisal or disbelief.

- **Social Norms and Cultural Contexts:** Broader societal norms and cultural attitudes towards gender, sexuality, and power can create an environment that either inhibits or facilitates sexual violence. Cultures that normalize male dominance, objectify women, or have weak legal and social sanctions against sexual assault can inadvertently contribute to a climate where such crimes are more likely to occur and less likely to be effectively addressed.

- **Lack of Protective Factors:** The absence of effective security measures, inadequate supervision, or a lack of bystander intervention can also create a facilitating environment. As seen in the Nirbhaya case, the failure of fellow passengers to intervene allowed the perpetrators to continue their assault unchecked.

4. **Influential Factors:** Shaping Attitudes and Behaviours

The final component of the Rapedemiological tetrad comprises the various "influential factors" that can shape attitudes, beliefs, and behaviours related to sexual violence within a society. These factors can contribute to the normalization, perpetuation, and even instigation of such acts:

- **Media and Pornography:** The pervasive influence of media, particularly the depiction of sexual violence in films and the widespread accessibility of pornography, warrants careful consideration. Exposure to violent or exploitative sexual content can desensitize individuals, normalize aggressive sexual behaviours, and, in vulnerable individuals, potentially contribute to the acting out of harmful fantasies. The shift towards increasingly explicit and readily available visual media has amplified this potential influence.

- **Social Discourse and Norms:** Casual conversations, jokes, and societal attitudes that trivialize sexual objectification, downplay the severity of sexual assault, or perpetuate victim-blaming narratives can contribute to a culture where such violence is more likely to occur and less likely to be effectively addressed.

- **Cultural Beliefs and Gender Inequality:** Deeply ingrained cultural beliefs about gender roles, power imbalances between men and women, and the objectification of women can create a societal context where sexual violence is more prevalent and less effectively challenged.

Understanding and addressing these influential factors is crucial for long-term prevention efforts that aim to shift societal attitudes, challenge harmful norms, and create a culture of respect and equality. Having laid this groundwork by dissecting the various elements that converge to create the conditions for sexual violence, the subsequent chapters will now turn a focused lens onto the second critical component of this tetrad: the perpetrators themselves. By exploring the diverse characteristics, motivations, and psychological underpinnings of male rapists, we aim to further unravel the complexities of this crime and inform more effective strategies for prevention and intervention.

Chapter 19

Unmasking the Predator: Characteristics of Male Perpetrators

A significant body of research has been devoted to examining the common characteristics of male perpetrators who sexually assault female victims. A deeper understanding of the characteristics most frequently associated with sexual assault perpetrators is useful in understanding the ethology of sexual assault perpetration and may be useful for identifying possible methods of intervention and prevention. These characteristics can be grouped into several broad categories:

- historical/developmental factors, including childhood abuse and sexual behaviour
- individual characteristics, including interpersonal skills and cognitions
- contextual factors, including perceptions of peer attitudes/behaviour and alcohol/drug use.

Historical/Developmental Factors

Childhood abuse, sexual abuse, physical abuse, emotional abuse, and exposure to violence within the home, has often been purported to be related to sexual assault perpetration later as an adult. A link between childhood abuse and later problems in adulthood, such as functioning in adult interpersonal relationships, substance abuse, depression, suicide, and various forms of violent behaviour, has been established. The insidious impact of childhood maltreatment can leave deep scars that manifest in a multitude of maladaptive behaviours in later life, and the perpetration of sexual assault is one particularly devastating outcome.

1. Childhood Sexual Abuse: At baseline, individuals who experienced sexual assault as a child were six times more likely to also have a history of engaging in sexually aggressive behaviour. The **victim-to-victimizer theory** posits that exposure to sexual abuse as a child leads the victim to reenact that childhood trauma as an adult on victims of his or her own.

This is not a simple case of imitation, but a complex psychological process where the abused child may internalize feelings of powerlessness, anger, and a distorted understanding of sexual interactions. As they mature, these unresolved traumas can manifest as a need to exert power and control over others, potentially through sexual violence, in a misguided attempt to process their own victimization. Studies have shown that sexual offenders against adults are more likely than sex offenders against children to have suffered child physical abuse, and sexual offenders against children are more likely than sex offenders against adults to have been sexually abused as children, suggesting a potentially nuanced relationship between the type of childhood abuse and the type of later offending.

The traumatic experiences of childhood abuse and the associated **lack of humane treatment** decrease the ability to empathize with others as adults, hindering the development of crucial inhibitions against harming others. Bolstering researchers' hypothesis that child sexual abuse more strongly predicts childhood molestation, in one study, childhood sexual abuse did not predict perpetration of assault against adult victims; rather, offenders who reported childhood sexual abuse and childhood exposure to pornography were less empathetic to child victims and reported perpetrating sexual abuse toward more child victims.

2. Childhood Physical Abuse: Studies have found that a high number of sexual assault perpetrators report experiencing abuse as a child. The traumatic experiences of childhood abuse and the associated lack of humane treatment decreases victims' ability to empathize with others as adults. Incarcerated offenders who self-reported childhood physical abuse were less empathetic to female victims and reported perpetrating sexual assault against more adult victims. Researchers have posited that subjection to physical violence as a child establishes a pattern of violence in interpersonal relationships. This early exposure to physical aggression can normalize violence as a means of resolving conflict and exerting control. Researchers have hypothesized that these experiences in early childhood may instil sexual interests that involve coercion or force, potentially linking the experience of being overpowered with sexual arousal in a distorted way. Boys subjected to physical violence in the home are more likely to later be arrested for a violent sex crime.

3. Childhood Emotional Abuse: According to the CDC, childhood emotional abuse includes behaviours that harm a child's self-worth or emotional well-being, such as name-calling, shaming, rejection, withholding love, or threats. Although this form of abuse is neither physical nor sexual, it can deeply damage a child's sense of self and their ability to form healthy relationships. Exposure to emotional abuse in childhood is linked to negative effects including heightened anger, irritability, and challenges in adult relationships marked by insecurity and mistrust. Research indicates that individuals who perpetrate sexual assault as adults are more likely to have experienced childhood emotional abuse compared to nonsexual offenders. This suggests that the deep harm to emotional regulation and interpersonal skills caused by such abuse can increase the risk of later committing sexual violence.

4. Childhood Exposure to Family Violence: Exposure to family violence is also associated with youth violence and violence as an adult. Witnessing violence between parents or other family members can desensitize children to aggression and normalize it as a way of interacting. One study found that witnessing domestic violence during childhood was predictive of committing both sexual and physical assault against an intimate partner. The researchers conclude that childhood victimization, including witnessing violence in the home, and sexual assault perpetration during adolescence may be precursors to sexual violence as young adults, with the effects of exposure to family violence indirectly affecting sexual assault perpetration by having an effect on adolescent behaviour, potentially through the adoption of violent conflict resolution styles and the development of hostile attitudes. Another line of research has established a link between individuals' prior sexual behaviour and the likelihood of adult sexual aggression.

Below, we describe some of the most frequently studied sexual behaviours, including number of sex partners, early initiation of sex, **impersonal or casual attitudes toward sex**, and past sexual violence perpetration.

5. Multiple Partners and Early Initiation of Sex: Correlation has been established between multiple sexual partners and/ or early initiation of sex and self-reported perpetration of sexual violence. These factors may be related to sexual assault perpetration because these individuals have a high degree of interest in sex and because the frequency of sexual experiences provides more opportunities to engage in sexually coercive behaviours. Early sexualization and a high number of partners might also be indicative of a lack of respect for sexual boundaries and a focus on sexual conquest.

6. Casual Attitudes Toward Sex: Studies have also identified a significant link between impersonal attitudes toward sex (defined as practices and beliefs that sex outside a relationship is acceptable) and sexual assault perpetration. Men with impersonal attitudes toward sex prefer casual sexual encounters to committed relationships and are motivated to have sex for sexual gratification rather than to feel intimacy or emotional closeness. This perspective can lead to the objectification of others and a disregard for their autonomy and consent. A casual attitude toward sex is also likely related to having multiple partners, therefore providing more opportunities to use coercive tactics to obtain sex.

Men with impersonal attitudes toward reindicated, for example, by endorsing statements such as “sex without love is OK”, are more likely to admit to commit sexual assault perpetration. This reflects a devaluation of emotional connection in sexual encounters, potentially making it easier to rationalize or engage in coercive behaviour.

7. Past Sexual Violence Perpetration: A history of sexual assault perpetration has been found to be associated or predictive of additional sexual assault perpetration, meaning that sexually aggressive men are likely to offend multiple times. This highlights the importance of early identification and intervention with individuals who have already engaged in sexually abusive behaviour.

Individual Characteristics:

Perpetrators are likely to display deficits in their interpersonal skills, including social-skill **deficits, empathetic deficits, and intimacy/attachment issues** in their personal relationships. During developmental years, individuals develop bonds that provide the foundation for pro-social, intimate relationships as adults. When this foundation is absent, individuals may try to experience intimacy inappropriately. Individuals may perpetrate sexual assault to achieve sexual gratification to compensate for difficulties they experience interacting with members of the opposite sex. Social-skill deficits may be more prevalent among child molesters than among adult sexual assault perpetrators.

1. Empathy Deficits: Perpetrators often lack empathy, or the ability to relate to someone else’s feelings. This inability to understand and share the emotional experience of another person is a significant factor in their capacity to inflict harm.

Sexual assault perpetrators exhibit lower levels of empathy toward victims of sexual assault than non-offenders, making it easier for them to disregard the victim's distress and focus solely on their own desires.

2. Attachment: Attachment theories assert the necessity of forming emotional bonds to others during the formative years, particularly during adolescence. Secure attachments provide a foundation for trust, intimacy, and healthy relationships. If these bonds are disrupted or absent, individuals develop insecure attachment styles characterized by fear of intimacy, difficulty trusting others, and a struggle with emotional regulation. Individuals with insecure attachments to others fail to develop necessary components for intimate adult relationships (for example, interpersonal skills and self-confidence), which in turn can lead to sexual aggression as a maladaptive way to seek connection or exert control.

3. Sexual Misinterpretation: Sexually aggressive men are more likely than nonaggressive men to misperceive a woman's friendliness as a sign of sexual interest. This **cognitive distortion** can lead to feelings of entitlement and anger when their perceived expectations are not met. A man who misinterprets initial interactions with a woman as indicative of sexual interest may feel led on at the point when a woman's actual disinterest becomes clear, which leads him to become angry and violent as a way to punish the perceived rejection and reassert control.

4. Gender-Related Attitudes and Cognitions: A number of gender-related attitudes and cognitions are related to an increased likelihood of committing sexual assault, including negative thoughts and attitudes toward women **(hostility**

toward women), ideologies about gender roles and masculinity **(belief in traditional gender roles, hypermasculinity, hostile masculinity)**, and misperceptions about women's role in sexual assault **(rape myth acceptance)**. The role of gender-related attitudes and cognitions has been among the most-studied factors in the sexual assault perpetration research, in part because rape is often conceptualized as an expression of anger against women or a method of obtaining dominance and control over women.

5. Hostility Toward Women: Men who express hostile attitudes toward women are more likely to commit sexual assault. This can manifest as misogynistic beliefs, a sense of entitlement over women, and a tendency to view women as objects. Studies have shown that using alcohol before or during sexual intercourse mediated the relationship between hostile attitudes toward women and sexual aggression, suggesting that alcohol can lower inhibitions and amplify pre-existing hostile tendencies.

6. Rape Myth Acceptance: Rape myths are defined as commonly held misperceptions that provide justification for rape, for example, the endorsement of beliefs that women unconsciously desire to be raped or beliefs that women who dress provocatively are asking to be raped. These myths serve to blame victims and absolve perpetrators of responsibility, creating a cognitive environment that normalizes or excuses sexual violence.

7. Belief in Traditional Gender Roles: Studies have also examined a link between beliefs in traditional gender roles (that women and men should adhere to their respective traditional roles and traits) and sexual assault perpetration. These beliefs often involve power imbalances and the objectification of women. Some studies have found a link between men in the general population who admit to having committed sexual assault and the endorsement of traditional gender roles. In another study, belief in traditional gender roles was the only significant predictor of sexual aggression when perceived token resistance (or reporting past sexual experiences in which the partner initially said he or she did not want to engage in sexual activity but eventually did) was included in the model. In this model, perceived token resistance and belief in traditional gender roles explained about 9 percent of the variance in whether someone engaged in sexually aggressive behaviour or not, highlighting how the belief that "no really means yes" can contribute to coercive behaviour.

8. Hypermasculinity: Hypermasculine men have been conceptualized as possessing callous attitudes toward sex, experiencing excitement in the face of danger, and believing that expression of violence is manly. These characteristics then predispose hypermasculine men to exert power and dominance over women, including exhibitions of sexual aggression. A number of studies have found an association between hypermasculinity and sexual assault perpetration. Hypermasculine men are more likely to display aggression toward women who violate traditional gender norms, suggesting that hypermasculine men may be compelled to assert their dominance when they feel their masculinity has been threatened, in this case, through challenges to traditional gender roles.

9. Hostile Masculinity: Hostile masculinity is defined as the need to control and dominate women, combined with hostility toward and distrust of women. It was found to be a significant pathway to sexual violence in a model of sexual aggression.

Men who reported the highest levels of hostile masculinity were most likely to have perpetrated sexual violence. This construct combines both negative attitudes and a drive for dominance, creating a particularly dangerous mindset.

Contextual Factors

Individuals who report having friends who engage in sexual aggression are more likely to then perpetrate sexual assault themselves. This highlights the influence of social norms and peer influence on behaviour. Individuals who perceive their peers as approving of sexual assault are more likely to commit sexual assault themselves, suggesting that a social environment that condones or normalizes sexual violence can significantly increase the likelihood of perpetration.

1. Alcohol: Research on the role of alcohol consumption in sexual assault perpetration has focused on two different mechanisms through which alcohol can have an effect: **pharmacological and psychological.** Pharmacological mechanisms of alcohol consumption refer to a decrease in cognitive functioning due to alcohol consumption and to a decrease in inhibitions. After consuming alcohol, individuals lose sight of distal cues, such as empathy for the victim and the long-term consequences of their actions, and focus instead on more immediate cues, such as sexual arousal, anger, and frustration. This effect has been theorized to be more likely in men who are predisposed to sexual aggression. Psychological mechanisms of alcohol consumption refer to the interaction between perpetrators' beliefs about the effects of alcohol on their own behaviour and the pharmacological effects of alcohol. In this respect, alcohol can affect how intoxicated individuals interpret behaviour around them to conform to what they want to happen. For example, if an individual is looking to engage in sex, they may interpret a woman's willingness to dance as an invitation to have sex, a misinterpretation fuelled by both intoxication and pre-existing desires.

2. Drug Use: The Malur case highlights that an intoxicated or high person may not know what he is actually doing; he may kill a woman without even raping her. While this specific example focuses on homicide, it underscores the broader point that drug use can severely impair judgment, reduce inhibitions, and lead to unpredictable and violent behaviour, including sexual assault.

This ties into broader theoretical frameworks that seek to explain why some individuals perpetrate sexual violence.

The Confluence Model is one of the most frequently cited and tested theories of adult sexual assault perpetration within the recent literature. The Confluence Model considers developmental, attitudinal, and environmental factors and describes two pathways to sexual aggression, the **hostile-masculinity pathway** and **the impersonal-sex pathway.**

The hostile-masculinity pathway describes a series of events in which an individual who experiences violence during childhood through abuse and parental violence begins to associate with delinquent peers. Association with delinquent peers then leads to development of negative attitudes toward women and romantic relationships and to beliefs that women are sexual objects.

The impersonal-sex pathway explains how abusive experiences at home can lead individuals to associate with delinquent peers who promote sexual promiscuity and conquests. This environment encourages early sexual activity, which in turn increases the chances of committing sexual assault. However, no single risk factor alone strongly predicts sexual assault perpetration. Instead, a wide range of factors collectively contribute to the risk, making prediction complex. To assist in this challenge, some countries have developed specialized tools, such as the Violence Risk Scale-Sex Offender Version (VRS-SO) and the Static-99, which criminal-justice professionals use to assess the likelihood of future offenses and inform their decisions.

Several different types of factors have been found to be associated with sexual assault perpetration. These include historical factors, such as abuse during childhood and prior sexual behaviour; individual-level factors, such as gender-related attitudes and cognitions; and contextual factors, such as peer influences and alcohol and drug use. The wide range of factors identified thus far illustrates the complexity of sexual assault perpetration. To date, no single factor has been found to be highly predictive of sexual assault perpetration; combinations of these factors interact in a number of different ways to influence sexual assault perpetration.

There are likely significant challenges associated with the development of a screening tool that could reliably identify individuals within the general population who are at risk to perpetrate sexual assault. The multifaceted nature of this crime and the ethical considerations surrounding prediction make this a complex and ongoing area of research

Chapter 20

The Shadow of the Screen: Porno Factor

While the causes of sexual crime are multifaceted and deeply rooted in complex psychological, social, and cultural factors, the pervasive and increasingly accessible nature of **pornography** warrants serious consideration as a significant contributing influence. To understand its potential impact, it is essential to first establish a working definition.

For the purpose of this discussion, **pornography** can be defined as **visual or textual material whose primary intention is to cause sexual arousal in the viewer or reader through the explicit depiction of sexual acts, body parts, or scenarios.** This definition encompasses a wide range of media, including videos, images, and written narratives, and distinguishes it from erotica, which may explore sexual themes in a more artistic or literary context with a less direct focus on explicit arousal. While the line between erotica and pornography can be subjective and debated, our focus here is on material that explicitly depicts sexual acts and/or genitalia with the primary goal of eliciting a sexual response.

With this definition in mind, we can now delve into the ways in which pornography, particularly its often-unrealistic, exploitative, and sometimes violent content, can contribute to the development of harmful attitudes, desensitization, and potentially, the perpetration of sexual offenses. It is crucial to state that pornography is not the sole cause of sexual crime, and attributing blame solely to its consumption would be an oversimplification. However, the evidence suggests a concerning correlation and potential causal pathways that demand careful scrutiny.

While pornography is not the sole cause of sexual crime, and blaming it entirely would oversimplify the issue, the evidence reveals a troubling connection that warrants careful examination.

One of the primary concerns surrounding widespread pornography consumption is its potential to erode empathy and normalize exploitative or dehumanizing portrayals of sexual interactions. Frequent exposure to content where individuals are treated as objects for gratification, where consent is often ambiguous or absent, and where power imbalances are fetishized can gradually desensitize viewers to the real-world implications of such dynamics. This desensitization can lead to a diminished capacity for understanding and appreciating the emotional and physical boundaries of others, a crucial component of healthy sexual relationships and respect for individual autonomy.

The constant consumption of pornography that often prioritizes the gratification of the viewer over the well-being and agency of the performers can cultivate a sense of entitlement and expectation in some individuals. This can manifest as a belief that sexual partners are primarily there to fulfil their desires, potentially leading to a disregard for consent and the imposition of unwanted sexual acts. The "stolen food" analogy, while simplistic, highlights this concern: if one's primary source of sexual stimulation depicts a disregard for boundaries and consent, the lines between fantasy and acceptable real-world behaviour can become dangerously blurred.

Building on this, pornography frequently depicts an idealized and unrealistic version of sexual encounters. The focus on performance, exaggerated physical attributes, and the absence of the emotional complexities inherent in real-life intimacy can create unattainable standards for viewers' own sexual experiences and partners. This can lead to dissatisfaction in real relationships, fostering a sense of inadequacy and potentially contributing to frustration and resentment that, in extreme cases, could manifest as aggression. The inability to reconcile the hyper-sexualized and often performative world of pornography with the nuances and imperfections of real-life intimacy can create a breeding ground for unrealistic expectations and potential conflict.

This concern becomes even more urgent when considering the consumption of violent pornography, which frequently depicts non-consensual acts, degradation, and the infliction of pain for sexual arousal. Research has consistently shown a correlation between exposure to violent pornography and an increase in attitudes supporting sexual aggression, as well as a potential increase in aggressive behaviour in general. The repeated exposure to such content can normalize violence within a sexual context, desensitize viewers to the suffering of victims, and potentially prime individuals with pre-existing aggressive tendencies to act on those impulses. Studies have even indicated that individuals with criminal histories are more likely to engage in sexual offenses after viewing violent pornography, suggesting a potential triggering effect.

Furthermore, non-violent pornography that still objectifies and dehumanizes individuals, particularly women, can contribute to a broader cultural context where the violation of their autonomy is more easily rationalized. By consistently portraying individuals as mere objects for sexual gratification, pornography can erode the perception of them as fully human beings deserving of respect and agency, making it easier for some individuals to disregard their rights and boundaries.

The increasing accessibility of pornography to children and adolescents is a particularly alarming trend. Developing minds are highly susceptible to the messages and portrayals they are exposed to, and early and frequent exposure to pornography can shape their understanding of sex, relationships, and consent in potentially harmful ways. This early exposure can contribute to the normalization of unrealistic expectations, the objectification of others, and a skewed understanding of healthy sexual development and intimacy. The potential long-term effects on attitudes towards sex and relationships in this digitally native generation warrant significant concern and further research.

Adding to this, peer pressure and online social norms can significantly influence pornography consumption, particularly among adolescents. The normalization of pornography use within peer groups can lead to increased exposure and acceptance, potentially desensitizing individuals at a crucial stage of their sexual development. This collective exposure can contribute to a shared understanding of sex that is heavily influenced by the often-distorted realities presented in pornography, further shaping attitudes and expectations.

While pornography, defined as explicit material intended for sexual arousal, is undoubtedly a complex phenomenon with varying interpretations and impacts, the evidence suggests that its widespread consumption, particularly of content that is unrealistic, exploitative, or violent, can contribute to a constellation of factors that may increase the risk of sexual crime. By potentially eroding empathy, normalizing exploitation, cultivating unrealistic expectations, and, in the case of violent pornography, potentially increasing aggressive tendencies, pornography can contribute to a cultural landscape where the violation of sexual boundaries is more likely to occur.

It is crucial to avoid simplistic causal links and acknowledge the multifaceted nature of sexual offending. However, dismissing the potential influence of such a pervasive and powerful medium would be irresponsible. A comprehensive approach to preventing sexual crime must include critical media literacy education, efforts to challenge harmful portrayals of sex and relationships, and a broader societal commitment to fostering empathy, respect, and a clear understanding of consent. Recognizing pornography as a potential contributing factor, alongside other psychological, social, and cultural influences, is a necessary step towards developing more effective strategies for preventing sexual violence and creating a safer society for all.

DREAM ANGEL
FOR EVERY
BOYS...

Chapter 21

The Shadow of the Screen

Pornography, a significant industry with a profound impact on sexual life, has undergone a dramatic evolution. Initially introduced through occasional adult movies on national television, followed by sporadic theatres showcasing adult films advertised with erotic posters, it gradually infiltrated the mainstream. The scale of the industry is now undeniable, with some pornographic websites even listed on the Stock Exchange. While defining and classifying erotic material remains a subject of debate, our focus here is on what is commonly understood as porn: videos depicting copulating organs in various permutations and combinations.

As the population adjusted to late-night adult movies, pornographic VHS and video cassettes made a significant entry. Entrepreneurial individuals even established businesses showing pornographic movies for a small fee in villages and towns during late hours in abandoned houses. Consequently, seemingly decent family men began watching Western sex videos. Movie theatres that had once survived on clandestine "A" grade "Sex" movies faced tough competition. The revolutionary debut of CD/DVDs led to the decline of veteran cassettes and theatres. Primitive smartphones with memory cards became popular among porn enthusiasts. Later, smartphones and the internet effectively replaced these earlier forms, and some early adopters remain leaders in adult entertainment. Alarmingly, not only adults but even children are now viewing explicit content, marking a revolutionary shift in entertainment, or rather adult entertainment, with a profound impact, especially in conservative countries like India.

The recent introduction of pornography via digital platforms has had a profound influence. As India was just recovering from state-sponsored midnight adult movies – a concept that still seems paradoxical in a densely populated country – the evolution of mobile phones led to a shift from memory cards with pornographic content to online pornography. Mobile repair shops in many places served as unofficial porn upload centres. A small shop could not solely rely on mobile accessory sales; under the guise of antivirus installation or minor repairs, customers would request explicit clips. Some shop owners had regular customers who would return for new videos after becoming familiar with the old ones over a week or two. Some uneducated individuals would even ask for "Chexx filims," mispronouncing "sex films" or "porn." Approximately 10 uploads a day at 100 rupees each provided a good income for small-village shops. Some shop owners even mentioned police personnel visiting to fill their mobiles with the latest videos. This offline business thrives in many villages with lower levels of education. Even uneducated farmers and labourers have explicit videos on their small mobile phones.

Online porn libraries cater to the educated, offering a choice of content ranging from simple videos to various perversions, with each site categorizing different types. When a sexually curious young boy starts watching porn, he will search for content that interests him. This means that group sex videos, sadistic, and masochistic videos can trigger various thoughts. The process of accepting porn often begins with the guilt of watching, evolving into a mental tolerance for the inhumane treatment of women. This can later progress to justifying such acts and potentially attempting similar behaviour if given the chance or opportunity.

While the vast majority of individuals who consume pornography would never perpetrate such violence, it is crucial to acknowledge the potential pathways through which its pervasive influence can, in a complex interplay of factors, sadly contribute to the heinous act of rape.

One major concern with pornography is the unrealistic expectations and distorted views it can create about sex and relationships. Like a "culinary show" offering an exaggerated and often exploitative menu of idealized bodies, performances, and scenarios, pornography frequently downplays or even ignores the vital importance of enthusiastic consent. Sexual encounters are often shown as forceful, submissive, or purely transactional, which can erode the understanding that sex must be a mutually desired and freely agreed-upon act. Repeated exposure to these portrayals can make viewers less sensitive to respecting boundaries and the essential need for willing participation, laying the groundwork for sexual coercion and violence.

Pornography also tends to reduce people, especially women, to objects valued only for their physical appearance and capacity to provide sexual pleasure. This dehumanization can make it easier for some individuals to dismiss others' feelings, rights, and humanity, creating a psychological distance that lowers inhibitions against harming them. When people are seen as objects rather than full human beings, violating them may feel less wrong in the minds of perpetrators.

Moreover, certain types of pornography explicitly depict aggression, domination, and coercion as sexually exciting. Frequent exposure to such content can normalize these behaviours for vulnerable viewers, blurring fantasy and reality. This dangerous belief that forces and manipulation are acceptable, or even desirable, aspects of sex can fuel violent tendencies.

Adding to these concerns is pornography's often addictive nature. Compulsive viewing may drive a craving for more extreme and violent material, deepening desensitization and reinforcing distorted ideas about sex and relationships. This cycle can dull empathy and make it harder to recognize the suffering of others.

Studies have shown that exposure to both violent and non-violent pornography can increase attitudes supporting sexual aggression as well as aggressive behaviour itself. For example, offenders have been found to be more likely to commit sexual acts like rape after watching porn. Although this does not mean pornography causes sexual violence for everyone, it signals a troubling correlation and a possible trigger for those already vulnerable or lacking empathy and respect.

Peer pressure and online social behaviours among adolescents further complicate the picture. Easy access to pornography via smartphones combined with consumption within peer groups can shape young people's developing ideas about sex and relationships. The normalization of aggression or non-consensual acts in these online circles can reinforce harmful attitudes early on.

It is important to stress that pornography viewing does not automatically result in sexual assault. Most people who consume pornography do not commit sexual violence. However, for a subset of individuals, especially those with pre-existing vulnerabilities, aggressive tendencies, or poor empathy, pornography can contribute to eroding respect for consent, normalizing objectification and aggression, and lowering inhibitions, thus creating a dangerous path toward sexual violence.

Understanding this complex relationship, recognizing how pornography's increasing accessibility influences attitudes, and acknowledging its potential role in fostering harmful views are essential steps in addressing its impact. This requires a multi-layered approach involving education, critical media literacy, and a societal commitment to promoting respect, empathy, and a clear understanding of consent.

In societies where movies and media are often taken as truth, it is unsurprising that pornography may be similarly absorbed and normalized, shaping social attitudes in powerful ways. Exploring how pornography becomes part of socialization is therefore crucial in tackling these challenges

Chapter 22

The Socialization of Pornography: Where Reel Life Warps Reality

In a country where cinema often blurs the lines between fiction and truth, where on-screen narratives can deeply influence societal perceptions, the pervasive presence of pornography takes on an even more concerning dimension. If movies are readily accepted as reflections of reality, it is no wonder that the often-distorted world of pornography might be received in a similar vein, shaping desires, expectations, and ultimately, behaviours in potentially damaging ways. Let's examine how this "socialization" of pornography unfolds.

The quiet hum of the small nursing home on that lazy afternoon was almost hypnotic. I was nearly dozing off in my consultation chair when the entrance door creaked open, and a well-built man in his late twenties stood before me. He seemed ordinary enough as he sat on the stool beside my desk, but his next words shattered the calm. "Sir," he began, his voice flat, "I have taken pills to commit suicide." There was no sign of intoxication or poisoning, just a stark declaration. "What pills, and how many?" I asked, my drowsiness instantly replaced by a surge of concern. "Around 100 CPM tablets," he replied, and then he broke down, and he began to sob, a deep, wrenching sound that echoed in the stillness of the room.

I explained the immediate need for a stomach wash and that further treatment would depend on the arrival of his relatives. But as soon as I mentioned family, his tears intensified. "No one will come, sir," he sobbed, "not even my wife." It was then that the pieces began to fall into place, suggesting a deeper marital issue beneath the surface of his despair.

As I gently probed further, a disturbing story unfolded. He had been assaulted, beaten black and blue, by his own father-in-law, a police officer. The reason, when it finally came, was startling. His wife, it turned out, had little to no interest in sexual intimacy. In a misguided attempt to bridge this gap and perhaps ignite some passion, he had shown her pornography. Her reaction was not what he expected; instead, she complained to her father, who responded with violence, dragging him to a police lockup and inflicting a brutal beating. I felt a profound sense of helplessness, caught in a situation that extended far beyond my medical capabilities. All I could do was refer him to a government facility, where he could receive the necessary psychiatric care and hopefully initiate some form of legal recourse.

This tragic case starkly illustrates how the consumption of pornography can be misinterpreted and mishandled within a social context. The husband, perhaps influenced by the hyper-sexualized portrayals in pornography, may have genuinely believed it could bridge the intimacy gap with his wife. However, his wife's reaction and her father's violent response highlight a severe disconnect in understanding and expectations, potentially fuelled by differing cultural norms and interpretations of sexual content. In a society where media can be readily accepted as truth, the husband's attempt to introduce pornography into his relationship backfired catastrophically, leading to violence and immense personal suffering.

This was not an isolated incident in my practice. I've seen other couples grapple with the impact of pornography on their relationships. Sometimes, they watch it together, and it only becomes a problem when other cracks appear in their bond. But in other cases, the influence is far more insidious. I remember a teenage boy, lost in the world of online pornography, who would watch it openly in the presence of his mother and sister. They were aware of his habit but never confronted him. The consequences were devastating: one day, he attempted to rape his sister and was caught. This tragic event starkly illustrated the dangerous potential of unchecked exposure to pornography, especially in young, developing minds, where the lines between the virtual and the real can be dangerously blurred. If the distorted power dynamics and lack of consent often depicted in pornography are internalized as normal or acceptable, the risk of acting out such behaviours in real life, particularly towards vulnerable individuals, increases alarmingly.

At the other end of the spectrum, some individuals delve so deeply into this world that they begin to create their own content, even engaging in and filming acts of self-copulation a truly shameful descent, indicative of a profound disconnect from healthy sexuality and social norms. The reach of pornography seems boundless, even extending into the halls of power. I've heard whispers, though unconfirmed, of lawmakers indulging in these videos during parliamentary sessions and even the disturbing practice of creating compromising, pornographic deepfakes of political rivals for blackmail. The potential for misuse, particularly in a politically charged environment where misinformation can spread rapidly, seems endless. If fabricated pornographic content can be used to tarnish reputations and exert influence, it further underscores the dangerous ways in which the distorted realities of pornography can bleed into real-world social and political dynamics.

Even in the mundane corners of everyday life, the pervasive influence of pornography is visible. I recall seeing an auto-rickshaw, a common sight here, adorned with a picture on its hood. It was a photograph of a woman, described as a " spectacled porn actress," and beneath it, the bold claim: "She is everyone's dream girl." I even took a picture of it, a stark reminder of how deeply these images have permeated our culture, shaping and perhaps distorting perceptions of desire and beauty. In a society where such blatant displays are commonplace, the constant exposure to idealized and often unrealistic portrayals of sexuality can subtly but powerfully influence what is considered desirable and normal, potentially contributing to dissatisfaction and unrealistic expectations in real-life relationships.

These fragmented encounters, these glimpses into the lives touched and sometimes shattered by pornography, paint a sobering picture of a complex and often damaging phenomenon. In a cultural context where media holds significant sway, the uncritical consumption of pornography, with its inherent distortions and potential for desensitization, carries a heightened risk of shaping harmful attitudes and behaviours, ultimately contributing to a societal landscape where the lines between fantasy and reality become dangerously blurred, with devastating consequences for individuals and relationships.

Chapter 23

Wild Web of Personal Pornography

The digital age has blurred the lines between the private and the public, creating new avenues for both intimacy and exploitation. The ease with which individuals can now create and share personal content, including pornography, presents a complex landscape with significant ethical and social implications. This chapter delves into the darker aspects of self-produced pornography and the potent influence of peer pressure in shaping adolescents' online sexual behaviours.

The allure of capturing intimate moments for personal reference has led some amorous couples to film their own pornographic videos. Intended as private keepsakes for future enjoyment, these recordings, however, are fraught with the risk of unauthorized dissemination. Often, a breach of trust, typically by one of the individuals involved, leads to these private moments being thrust into the public domain. Tragically, the consequences of such leaks are often disproportionately severe for the female partner. While the male partner may, in some instances, gain a degree of notoriety, the female individual frequently faces devastating repercussions, including social ostracization, profound shame, and, in the most heartbreaking cases, even suicide, after the videos are viewed by close relatives and friends. This stark reality underscores the vulnerability inherent in creating and storing such personal content and the potential for irreparable harm when privacy is violated. Furthermore, this vulnerability can be exploited, leading some women into a vicious cycle of exploitation for sex, money, and other Favors, trapped by the potential threat of their private content being made public.

Beyond consensual couple-produced content, a more sinister form of personal pornography involves exploitation and the violation of trust. A disturbing recent case highlighted this darker aspect, where an outwardly ordinary young boy was suspected of filming several thousand sex videos of himself by luring unsuspecting and innocent women. This illustrates a predatory dynamic where individuals exploit others, often through deception or coercion, to create their own personal pornographic material. This form of self-produced pornography is not about shared intimacy but about the objectification and violation of others for personal gratification, leaving victims traumatized and their trust shattered.

The digital landscape also serves as a powerful arena for peer pressure and the shaping of online sexual behaviour, particularly during adolescence. The American Psychological Association (APA) defines peer pressure as "the influence that peers can have on each other, which leads individuals to change their attitudes, values, or behaviours to conform to group norms." This phenomenon is particularly potent during the teenage years, a period marked by identity formation and the desire for social acceptance.

A significant global study revealed widespread online addiction, encompassing smartphones, social media, the internet, cybersex, and games, a trend exacerbated by the isolation imposed during the COVID-19 lockdowns. This increased online engagement during a critical developmental period had specific consequences for young people's sexual behaviour. The lockdowns saw a rise in online sexual activities among adolescents, including sharing nude pictures, engaging in exhibitionist behaviour on social media, and even participating in mutual masturbation via video calls. Notably, these behaviours were reported more frequently by young men than women in the study. In a country like India with a large and active internet user base, and a significant presence of online pornography, understanding these trends is crucial. Studies indicate that a considerable portion of men in India who use the internet access pornography on a daily basis, suggesting a normalization of its consumption.

Research examining the factors influencing sexual behaviour in adolescents has highlighted the interconnectedness of pornography use, peer pressure, and the home environment. While all these factors play a role, the dynamics within the home appear to be the most influential. Interestingly, studies suggest that boys and girls use mobile porn at roughly similar rates. However, boys are more likely to send naked or almost naked pictures. Factors such as popularity, feeling pressure from friends, and being older correlate with a higher likelihood of both sending such images and viewing pornography on their phones. Conversely, girls in younger grades are more likely to have pornography on their phones, indicating the significant influence of peer behaviour on their exposure. This underscores the powerful role that friends and social circles play in shaping adolescents' engagement with online sexual content.

Finally, the text alludes to common characteristics among individuals who perpetrate sexual harm but does not elaborate on these traits. It is important to note that while factors like exposure to pornography and peer influence can contribute to the development of harmful attitudes and behaviours in some individuals, they are part of a complex web of personal, social, and psychological factors that contribute to sexual violence. Understanding the interplay of these elements is crucial for developing effective prevention and intervention strategies. With all the above influences let's get deeper into the minds of perpetrators.

Chapter 24

Deconstructing the Offender

The assertion that rape is not a sexually motivated act, but rather driven by power, control, violence, and/or domination, has significantly influenced discussions surrounding sexual assault. This view sees the sexual aspect of rape as just a means to achieve other nonsexual goals. However, a closer look reveals that this explanation has flaws; it relies on narrow definitions, makes assumptions that don't hold up, and contradicts how rapists actually behave. Exploring the psychology of rapists helps clarify these complexities and challenges common misconceptions.

One key argument for the "not sex" theory is that sex only means consensual, romantic acts. But this ignores that sexual urges can exist without love or romance, as seen in many animal behaviours and human expressions of sexuality. Another claim says that rapists with partners aren't sexually motivated because sexual desire is limited. Yet, people regularly have sex outside their main relationships, which disproves this idea. Others argue that because some rapes are planned, they can't be sexually driven, but many consensual sexual encounters are also carefully planned.

Some say rape peaks at ages when violence is high but sexual drive isn't, suggesting it's about aggression alone. However, research shows sexual activity in men tends to peak and fall with age, which lines up with rape patterns, implying sex plays a role. During war, rape is often explained purely as hostility, but the vulnerability of women and use of pornography to arouse soldiers suggest sexual motivations mix with violence. Even using rape as a tool for social control doesn't mean sexual feelings aren't involved.

Rapists' own accounts complicate the picture: while many claim power and control as motives, they also admit sexual arousal, challenging the "not sex" claim. Redefining sex to exclude acts without victim arousal seems arbitrary. High rates of sexual dysfunction during rape have been cited as proof of no desire, but these rates vary and can be explained by stress, anxiety, and drugs. Others argue rape follows the same seasonal patterns as non-sexual violence, implying it's just aggression. But this ignores other factors and differences among violent crimes. Claims that castrated rapists redirect aggression non-sexually don't hold up, since castration reduces both sexual and general violent behaviour. Also, labelling rape as just violence with sex as a weapon often overlooks that some force is typical in sexual assault. Arguments claiming sex is just a tool for control are hard to test scientifically.

Contrary to stereotypes, many rapists are known to their victims, exploiting trust and familiarity. Rape is better understood as a violent crime where sex is the weapon, driven by a desire for power, control, and causing harm. It often stems from an inability to form healthy intimacy or obtain consent properly. Rather than spontaneous acts, rape is frequently premeditated, involving choosing and watching victims. Serial offenders are common and often show personality disorders like psychopathy or antisocial traits, with backgrounds of childhood trauma. The act itself can give disturbing pleasure, fuelled by sadistic fantasies and dehumanizing victims, helping perpetrators justify their actions.

Studies identify different types of rapists: those feeling socially or economically disadvantaged, sadistic offenders, opportunists, those who invest great effort in seeking new victims, and partners who commit sexual violence. Yet, a common thread is a deep sense of entitlement and a lack of respect for others' autonomy, often shaped by patriarchal cultures.

In the end, while the "not sex" explanation has highlighted important issues about victim trauma and societal influences, its main points have clear weaknesses. Evidence shows sexual motivation, often mixed with power and aggression, plays a central role. To effectively prevent and address sexual violence, we must understand the mindsets and motives of rapists, challenge stereotypes, recognize what drives their violence, and confront the complex psychological realities behind their actions. Doing so is key to tackling entitlement and promoting respect for individual autonomy.

Chapter 25

The Shadowed Paths: The Genesis

By examining below situations with a focus on realistic progression, we aim to understand the complex interplay of opportunity, power dynamics, individual choices, and the potential for the development of perverse desires.

The Woods Behind the Village: The Corrupting Gaze and the Descent into Predation

Two teenagers, seeking a clandestine escape from the mundane routines of village life, found themselves drawn to the secluded woods. An old, dilapidated bungalow became their initial haven, a place to experiment with their first cigarettes and share the tentative bravado of adolescence. One evening, their idle chatter stretched into the deepening twilight. The realization that they were not alone pierced their youthful reverie – hushed laughter, escalating into moans and amorous cries, drifted through the trees. Drawn by a mixture of curiosity and burgeoning sexual awareness, they cautiously approached the source of the sounds.

The scene illuminated by their flickering torch was both shocking and strangely compelling. A naked couple, villagers they knew, locked in the throes of passion in a secret, extramarital encounter. The woman, seemingly the epitome of piety within their community, was engaged in an act that defied their young understanding of social norms. The man, startled by the sudden intrusion, scrambled for his discarded pants and fled into the darkness. The woman, however, was more encumbered, the layers of her innerwear, saree, and blouse hindering a swift escape under the intense gaze of the two teenagers. Shame and fear flickered across her face as she pressed a wad of cash into their hands, a desperate attempt to buy their silence before hurrying away into the night.

The immediate reward of the money, coupled with the lingering thrill of witnessing the forbidden act, had an unforeseen effect on the boys. Their evenings in the woods took on a new purpose. The thrill of catching other illicit couples became a perverse game, their initial shock evolving into a calculated exploitation. They graduated from the nicotine buzz of cigarettes to the hazy intoxication of weed, their voyeurism fuelling a nascent and distorted sexual curiosity. The desire to merely observe waned, replaced by a craving to participate, to exert their own control in these clandestine encounters.

Armed with their torch, they devised a plan. They would intentionally startle couples, knowing the man would likely flee, leaving behind a vulnerable, naked woman in the darkness. Their interactions with these women took a disturbing turn. The torchlight, initially a tool of discovery, became an instrument of intimidation and objectification. They would slowly trace the contours of the woman's naked body, from her feet upwards, lingering on thighs and genitals before finally illuminating her face, revelling in her plight and vulnerability. This act of forced exposure became a prelude to sexual assault, a means of exerting power and silencing their victims. The boys, emboldened by their impunity and the fear they instilled, further exploited the women, demanding money and eventually even snatching gold jewellery. The threat of public exposure ensured their continued silence and availability for further exploitation.

This descent into sexual violence can be understood as a perversion of their initial curiosity, twisted by opportunity, a growing sense of power, and a profound desensitization to the humanity of their victims. Their actions, in their focus on the naked female form and the desire for control, echo, in a crude and brutal way, the unsettling world of sexual fetishism.

Consider, for instance, the disturbing case of Umesh Reddy, an Indian serial killer and rapist. Reddy harboured an intense and specific fixation on women's undergarments. His criminal history revealed a compulsive need to steal lingerie, often from the backyards of houses. He was repeatedly arrested while wearing women's undergarments beneath his own clothes, and his residence was found to contain a significant collection of these items. More chillingly, after raping and murdering his victims, Reddy would often take their undergarments as trophies. This act suggests a deep and perverse connection between his violent sexual urges and his fetish, the intimate apparel serving as a tangible symbol of his dominance and the violation he inflicted.

While the boys in the woods were not engaging in the same extreme acts of violence, their focus on the naked women, their ritualistic humiliation with the torchlight, and the subsequent sexual assaults indicated a disturbing development of perverse desires rooted in power, control, and the objectification of others. Their actions, fuelled by a sense of impunity and a growing disregard for their victims' autonomy, mirrored, in a nascent and localized way, the disturbing intersection of sexual fixation and harmful behaviour seen in cases like that of Umesh Reddy. The shocking climax, where they unwittingly target the mother of one of the boys, served as a brutal and unforeseen consequence of their twisted path, leading one down the dark spiral of drug addiction.

The Unconventional Desire: The Lingering Scent of the Forbidden

A young, affluent woman, experiencing what she described as an overwhelming surge of libido, found herself driven to seek immediate release in a setting far removed from the opulence of her privileged life: a dirty, malodorous public toilet. Her partner in this impulsive act was equally unexpected – her older, unshaven car driver. This first sexual encounter, amidst the grime and stench of the public restroom, defied all conventional notions of romance and sexual attraction.

Yet, this initial experience, marked by its raw and unrefined nature, left an indelible imprint on her developing sexuality. The sensory details of the encounter – the unpleasant smells, the rough touch, the sheer unexpectedness of it all – became inextricably linked to her arousal. This potent first experience perversely shaped her future desires, leading her to find herself no longer attracted to the sterile perfection of posh hotel rooms or the polished charm of conventionally handsome partners. Instead, she found herself drawn to similar unrefined and even repulsive settings, seeking to recapture the intensity of that initial, unconventional encounter. Her decision to write to a psychological counsellor for help reveals her own awareness of the unusual and potentially problematic nature of this developed perversion, a testament to the powerful and sometimes unexpected ways in which initial sexual experiences can shape lifelong desires.

The Field's Edge: The Banality of Cruelty and the Seeds of Twisted Pleasure

Two young men from a village encountered a lone woman working in her fully grown jowar field. In a swift and brutal act of dominance, one of the youths grabbed her saree, ripping it away and leaving her naked and exposed in the open field.

They then offered a chillingly pragmatic "deal": her clothes would be returned only if she complied. Under this coercion, the woman was forced to agree. This was a clear case of "so-called consensual rape," with no genuine consent present, only blatant coercion. The act was driven not by sexual desire but by a need for power and the thrill of subjugation.

Afterward, the youths were overheard boasting about their "memories" of the assault and recounting similar attacks on other women in the village. Their casual cruelty and the twisted pleasure they took in recounting these violations revealed a deeply ingrained perversion; an enjoyment derived from the degradation and domination of others. This incident highlights the disturbing presence of such dark desires within that community.

This stark anecdote underscores how a sense of power and impunity can lead to the development of a perverted enjoyment in inflicting sexual violence, completely detached from any genuine sexual desire. It reveals the dangerous dynamics where domination and control become the driving forces behind such acts, highlighting the urgent need to confront and address these deeply rooted attitudes within communities

Chapter 26

The Gazelle and the Gathering

In situations of extreme deprivation and crisis, the instinct to survive can drive individuals and communities to actions they might never otherwise consider. When basic needs like food and safety are threatened, desperation can push people into moral and psychological territory where the lines between survival and violence begin to blur. This chapter examines how hunger and collective hardship can not only lead to acts of violence but also transform the way individuals experience and relate to that violence.

Extended periods of hardship and scarcity place immense strain on both individuals and communities, wearing down not only their physical strength but also their spirit, sense of normalcy, and hope for the future. When the land stops providing, and familiar sources of food disappear, the struggle shifts beyond simple hunger, it becomes a profound psychological burden. The people affected begin to change, not only in body but in mind. Their conversations shorten, their eyes lose their sparkle, and a heavy air of desperation settles in. This growing dissatisfaction and stress begin to alter the way they think and interact with one another, breeding tension and reshaping social dynamics.

In such desperate environments, the arrival of a vulnerable animal, such as a gazelle wandering into the camp, represents more than a chance for nourishment. It embodies a test of instincts, morality, and communal will. For individuals weakened by prolonged hunger, the tension between compassion for a living creature and the imperative to survive presents a difficult dilemma. The initial hesitation before an act of violence is natural; the peaceful and trusting presence of the animal triggers a momentary pause. Yet, hunger's urgency often overwhelms this hesitation, pushing people to inflict harm not born from hatred but out of sheer necessity.

When one person acts, the instinct to survive spreads quickly through the group. Others, driven by the same hunger and desperation, join in, not because of premeditated plans but through shared understanding and impulse. This spontaneous cooperation transforms individual desperation into collective force. The cries of the wounded animal fade into the background, drowned out by the imperative to survive. Questioning the morality of the act becomes secondary to securing sustenance, and with survival on the line, the violence goes unchallenged and even becomes justified in the eyes of the group.

The impact of this violent act goes beyond its immediate physical outcome. It sparks a profound psychological shift within the individuals involved. The young man who struck first finds himself awakened to feelings he had not known for some time, both relief and a sense of power. For someone who had felt weak and powerless, this newfound control is intoxicating. This emotional change is reinforced by the group's approval, replacing guilt and hesitation with validation. Violence, which might have once seemed unthinkable or immoral, begins to feel natural and acceptable.

Over the days that follow, the young man's behaviour and outlook evolve. He sharpens his tools more frequently, watches the horizon with heightened alertness, and talks about the hunt with pride and accomplishment, no longer seeing it merely as a survival tactic but as an achievement. The killing of the gazelle feeds not just his body but also his ego. He begins to seek out the feeling it gave him again; the rush of dominance, the exhilaration of control. The boundary between acting out of need and acting out of desire blurs. Violence ceases to be merely a desperate means of survival; it becomes, increasingly, an end in itself.

This progression can be understood through several psychological frameworks. Operant conditioning explains that when behaviours are followed by immediate rewards, such as food or social approval, they are reinforced, which increases the likelihood of those behaviours being repeated. Desensitization, the gradual reduction in emotional sensitivity resulting from repeated exposure to violence, lowers the emotional barriers that normally inhibit harmful behaviour. Moral disengagement allows individuals to justify violence as necessary, enabling them to bypass feelings of guilt and moral responsibility. Additionally, group dynamics play a critical role: acting collectively diffuses personal accountability, making violent acts easier to carry out and more difficult to regret.

Together, these factors show how environmental pressures, social reinforcement, and psychological vulnerabilities can combine to transform a reluctant survivor into someone who begins to take satisfaction in violence. This transformation is not the result of an inherent or sudden evil impulse but rather a slow erosion of empathy, moral restraint, and personal identity caused by prolonged stress and desperation. It highlights the complex ways survival mechanisms, group influence, and human psychology intersect, revealing how violence can become ingrained and normalized under extreme conditions. Understanding this process is essential to addressing the root causes of violence and developing responses that consider both individual psychology and broader social context.

PART IV:
SCOPE & IMPACT

Chapter 27

Understanding Child Sexual Abuse

Child sexual abuse, also referred to as child molestation, constitutes a grave form of child abuse wherein an adult or an older adolescent exploits a child for their own sexual gratification. This exploitation can manifest in various ways, including direct sexual contact initiated through requests, pressure, or other manipulative tactics. It also encompasses indecent exposure, where the genitals are displayed inappropriately, the insidious process of child grooming aimed at lowering a child's defences and building trust for later abuse, and the abhorrent act of using a child to produce child pornography.

The settings in which child sexual abuse can occur are tragically diverse, ranging from the supposed safety of a child's own home to institutions like schools and even workplaces where child labour is prevalent. One particularly insidious and widespread form of child sexual abuse is child marriage. UNICEF has poignantly described child marriage as "perhaps the most prevalent form of sexual abuse and exploitation of girls," highlighting its devastating impact on young lives.

The consequences of child sexual abuse are profound and far-reaching, often leaving deep and lasting scars. Survivors may grapple with depression, the debilitating effects of post-traumatic stress disorder (PTSD), pervasive anxiety, and the complex constellation of symptoms known as complex PTSD. Tragically, the trauma of child sexual abuse can also increase an individual's vulnerability to further victimization in adulthood. Furthermore, children may suffer direct physical injury as a result of the abuse. When the abuse is perpetrated by a family member, it constitutes incest, a particularly damaging form of betrayal that can lead to even more severe and long-term psychological trauma, especially in cases involving parental incest.

Global estimates paint a stark picture of the prevalence of this crime, suggesting that approximately 19.7% of females and 7.9% of males have experienced child sexual abuse. This underscores the widespread nature of this issue and the urgent need for understanding and prevention.

Within this context, the term "child sexual abuser" broadly describes any individual who engages in the sexual abuse of minors. However, it is crucial to distinguish this term from the clinical diagnosis of "paedophilia." While the terms are often conflated in public discourse, they represent distinct concepts.

"Paedophile," in a clinical context, refers to an individual aged 16 years or older who, following a diagnosis by a qualified professional, experiences an exclusive or non-exclusive sexual attraction to prepubescent children, typically those under the age of 13, and who meets a specific set of diagnostic criteria. Notably, these diagnostic criteria have faced criticism, particularly the requirement that a person must have sexually abused children for a diagnosis of paedophilia to be made.

Despite this clinical definition, the term "paedophile" is frequently and mistakenly used by the general population to refer to anyone who sexually abuses children. In reality, only a minority of those who perpetrate child sexual abuse actually meet the diagnostic criteria for paedophilia. Research suggests that child sexual abusers who do meet the diagnostic criteria for paedophilia are more likely than non-paedophile abusers to have victimized younger individuals, males, and individuals outside their own family, and are also more likely to have abused multiple children.

Child sexual abusers are a diverse group with no single profile. They can be male or female, heterosexual, homosexual, or bisexual, and come from any ethnic or socio-economic background. They may be in relationships or single, reflecting the broad range of individuals who commit these offenses. While motivations for abuse vary, certain personal traits are found more frequently among offenders than non-offenders. These include poor social skills, strained or unsatisfactory relationships with adults, feelings of powerlessness, low self-esteem, vulnerability about masculinity, humiliation, loneliness, emotional attachment difficulties, and sexual problems.

However, it is important to stress that having these characteristics does not automatically label someone as an abuser or predict abusive behaviour; they are simply traits observed more often in offender groups. Understanding child sexual abuse also requires attention to factors such as the abuser's gender and age, their relationship to the victim, mental health, and cognitive distortions.

Criminal profiling has identified three distinct types of child sexual abusers: the "isolated paedophile," the "orderly paedophile," and the "festive paedophile." These profiles help law enforcement identify suspects and guide investigations, offering valuable tools for addressing this complex issue.

Research has illuminated the strategies that perpetrators often employ to commit child sexual abuse. Contrary to the assumption that physical force is the primary method, child sexual abusers rarely rely on physical coercion. Instead, many prioritize establishing an emotional relationship with the child, and this significantly shapes the tactics they use.

A significant majority of sexual offenses against children, estimated between 70% and 80%, are premeditated. This contradicts the notion that these acts are driven by uncontrolled impulses and a lack of self-control.

Perpetrators who abuse children from outside their family often strategically position themselves in roles of authority or access to unsupervised children. This might involve volunteering with children, coaching sports teams, or working in childcare settings. Their subsequent aim is to gain the trust of both the children and their parents.

Many children sexual abusers, often possessing poor social skills, find comfort in relationships with children who are passive, psychologically dependent, and easily manipulated. Indeed, these characteristics can make children more vulnerable to exploitation and are actively sought out by some perpetrators.

The majority of child sexual abusers cultivate an environment that erodes a child's resistance, paving the way for victimization. This preparatory phase involves manipulating potential victims into consenting to the sexual activities initiated by the abuser. Common strategies employed, most of which do not involve direct coercion, include: creating a state of emotional dependence and manipulation, seduction, persuasion and manipulation, the use of games, gradual desensitization, offering gifts and privileges, and, in some instances, resorting to threats or physical and verbal coercion.

Chapter 28

Roots of Rape, Mapping the Conditions That Enable Sexual Violence

Harmful sexual desire rarely emerges suddenly; it develops gradually, shaped by both inner vulnerabilities and external influences. Cultural narratives often link masculinity with dominance, aggression, and conquest. From a young age, boys are taught to equate strength with control and emotional distance with toughness. In this framework, sexuality becomes less about connection and more about asserting power. For men feeling powerless in other parts of their lives, sexual aggression may appear as one of the few areas where control can be claimed. This behaviour is not natural but constructed, revealing how deeply gender expectations can distort desire and intimacy into harmful forms.

Adding complexity, many perpetrators carry painful histories of childhood sexual abuse, sometimes inflicted by relatives or authority figures and occasionally by women, challenging common stereotypes. These cycles of harm reveal how unresolved trauma can be replayed on new victims, where motivations to harm arise less from sexual desire and more from rage, dissociation, and deep psychological wounds. Such individuals are not born predators but are shaped by harsh experiences. Yet this understanding is not an excuse but a call for urgent early intervention before trauma evolves into violence.

While personal psychology sets a foundation, culture strongly reinforces harmful patterns. Violent or non-consensual pornography blurs the boundaries between sex and aggression, conditioning arousal to align with domination and diminishing empathy. Mainstream media further fuels this by glamorizing male conquest and female submission, portraying coercion as flirtation and silence as consent. These messages seep deeply into the sexual imagination, shaping expectations around intimacy and power both consciously and unconsciously.

Most people have internal restraints such as moral, emotional, and psychological, that prevent harmful impulses from turning into action. However, factors like intoxication, peer pressure, narcissism, and dehumanization can erode these barriers. Cultural myths that treat women as always available or suggest "no" means "maybe" further break down these restraints. Such beliefs don't merely justify violence after it happens; they prepare the ground, dulling guilt and fostering a dangerous sense of entitlement.

When societal systems fail to hold offenders accountable, the risk increases. Law enforcement, courts, schools, and media often fail survivors while protecting perpetrators, dismissing cases, shifting blame, and denying justice. Some institutions such as the military, religious organizations, or elite schools, enforce silence under the guise of preserving honour or reputation, allowing rape to go unpunished. When perpetrators believe their actions carry little consequence, they treat sexual violence as negotiable. Survivors, faced with traumatization or barriers to justice, often remain silent, unintentionally reinforcing the false belief that such violence is rare or exaggerated.

Even when all other factors are present, one critical element remains: the victim's vulnerability. This vulnerability is often socially constructed rather than purely physical. Women are frequently socialized to be accommodating, non-confrontational, and emotionally available, sometimes at the expense of their own safety. Expressions of anger, suspicion, or resistance are discouraged, weakening natural defences. The fear of severe harm or death can freeze victims into compliance, often mistaken for consent. The closer the perpetrator is to the victim, the more confusing and paralyzing the response may become. Trust becomes a trap, and betrayal adds a painful layer to the violation.

These intertwined psychological, cultural, systemic, and interpersonal factors do not excuse rape, but they explain why it continues to persist. Addressing rape solely as a criminal act tackles only the surface and overlooks deeper causes. True prevention requires transformation, such as changing how boys are taught about power and consent, how trauma is addressed, how institutions are held accountable, and how women are empowered to resist rather than just survive. This is not about control but about rebuilding. Only by understanding this complex web of enabling conditions can society begin to dismantle the structures that make sexual violence possible.

Chapter 29

The Hidden Numbers, Factors Contributing to Underreporting

Global statistics on child sexual abuse, already deeply troubling, likely represent only a fraction of the true prevalence. A complex mix of psychological, social, cultural, and systemic factors contributes to widespread underreporting. Many survivors face enormous barriers that prevent them from speaking out, and these obstacles sustain a cycle of silence while blocking access to justice.

One of the most powerful barriers is the intense stigma and shame tied to victimization. Survivors often internalize society's harmful attitudes that wrongly blame them, leading to feelings of guilt, self-blame, and isolation. This is especially true in cultures where sexuality is taboo or victim-blaming is common. Children may fear being labelled "damaged" or "impure," and adults who suffered abuse in childhood may carry shame their entire lives, keeping them silent. Even when survivors know they are not at fault, the fear of judgment or rejection by family, friends, or society can be overwhelming. This internalized shame silences countless voices and delays or denies them access to support.

Fear of retaliation is another major reason for silence. The power imbalance in child sexual abuse often means the abuser holds authority, is a family member, or has social influence, making it even harder for victims to speak out. Children may be threatened directly or indirectly with punishment, harm to loved ones, or more abuse if they disclose. These fears are not without foundation. Survivors and their families may face intimidation, social exclusion, or even physical danger when trying to report abuse. This is particularly true in close-knit communities or families where the abuser is protected or respected. The constant threat of retaliation creates an environment of fear that keeps victims silent and allows abuse to continue unchecked.

Many cases go unreported simply because children do not recognize their experiences as abuse. Young children often lack the understanding or words to describe what happened and may feel confused, scared, or conflicted, especially if the abuser is someone they trust or love. Caregivers and educators can also miss signs of abuse due to lack of training, denial, or cultural beliefs. Subtle abuse like grooming, emotional manipulation, or coercion is especially hard to detect. In some families or communities, abuse is even normalized, making it invisible. Without proper awareness and education, children and adults alike may fail to understand what safe and respectful behaviour looks like, allowing abuse to persist quietly.

Even when children realize something is wrong, telling someone can be emotionally and psychologically difficult.

Limited language skills, confusion, or fear of disbelief can make disclosure a challenge. Children may feel loyalty to the abuser, especially if they are a family member. Sharing their experience can also retraumatize them, triggering intense emotions like fear, shame, and anxiety. They may worry about being blamed, punished, or separated from their family. These fears grow stronger if previous attempts to talk were met with disbelief or lack of protection. Because of this, many children stay silent, and those who do speak up often do so in fragmented or indirect ways that adults may miss or misunderstand.

Beyond these individual and social hurdles, systemic failures within law enforcement, legal systems, and institutions contribute heavily to underreporting. Many survivors and families simply do not trust that the justice system will treat their cases fairly or sensitively. Reporting processes often lack child-friendly approaches and fail to have trained professionals prepared to handle abuse disclosures, sometimes causing further trauma or discouragement. In some places, legal definitions of abuse are too narrow or outdated, excluding many forms of exploitation or coercion. Lengthy court procedures, lack of confidentiality, and few support services further discourage survivors from coming forward. Without meaningful reform, these systemic shortcomings will continue to block justice and keep survivors silent.

Together, these psychological, social, cultural, and institutional barriers create a complex web that hides much of the true scope of child sexual abuse. Breaking this silence requires more than awareness. It demands systemic change, education, sensitive support structures, and cultural shifts that empower survivors to come forward and find justice.

Chapter 30

The Enduring Scars, Consequences for Survivors

While some individuals who have experienced the trauma of child sexual abuse manage to navigate their lives with resilience and support, many face deep and lasting psychological distress. The wounds caused by such abuse often run far beneath the surface, leading to complex and debilitating mental health issues that may not fully emerge until years or even decades later.

One of the most significant effects is complex trauma, or Complex PTSD, which differs from the more commonly known PTSD by arising from prolonged or repeated trauma, such as ongoing abuse or neglect during childhood. Survivors often struggle with emotional regulation, experiencing intense and unpredictable feelings like chronic anger, sadness, fear, and shame that interfere with everyday life and relationships. Their self-perception can become deeply damaged, with persistent feelings of guilt, shame, and the belief that they are unworthy or broken. Trust becomes a major hurdle in relationships, as survivors may fear intimacy, avoid vulnerability, or repeat harmful patterns. Many even face a fragmented sense of self, feeling detached or struggling to maintain a cohesive identity.

Depression and anxiety are also common aftereffects. Survivors often battle persistent sadness or hopelessness, chronic worry or panic attacks, sleep problems, fatigue, and difficulty concentrating. These disorders can coexist with trauma symptoms, severely affecting their ability to work, maintain relationships, and enjoy life.

Dissociative disorders may develop as well, where survivors mentally escape from overwhelming trauma through defence mechanisms. This can lead to memory gaps, feelings of detachment from their body or surroundings, and in severe cases, fragmentation of identity with multiple personality states.

To numb their emotional pain or avoid intrusive memories, some survivors turn to substance abuse. Alcohol or drug use may offer temporary relief but ultimately worsens psychological distress and increases vulnerability. Addiction can also prevent survivors from seeking help due to fear of judgment or lack of trauma-informed care.

The betrayal of trust during abuse often creates lasting challenges in relationships. Survivors may fear emotional closeness, avoid expressing vulnerability, struggle to set healthy boundaries, or find themselves in relationships that mirror past abuse. These difficulties can trap survivors in cycles of isolation and emotional pain, complicating recovery.

Furthermore, survivors face a higher risk of being victimized again in adulthood. Eroded self-worth, learned helplessness, and difficulty setting boundaries can make them more vulnerable to exploitation in many settings. This vulnerability is not a sign of weakness but a direct consequence of trauma, highlighting the urgent need for early intervention, empowerment, and trauma-informed care to break the cycle and support healing.

Chapter 31

The Societal Fabric of Sexual Violence

Violence is rarely just a personal act. It is often a reflection of the wider social, cultural, and historical forces that shape our communities. While survival may drive certain violent behaviours, another form of violence, sexual violence, permeates societies worldwide in ways that are deeply rooted and systemic. This chapter exposes how sexual violence extends far beyond individual aggression, revealing its foundations in long-standing social norms, power structures, and institutional practices that continue to enable and perpetuate it.

This chapter examines how sexual violence is deeply embedded in the social fabric, perpetuated through language, institutions, and collective memory. It reveals that sexual violence is not just an individual act of aggression but a reflection of broader societal structures and cultural forces.

Language plays a powerful role in this perpetuation. Phrases like "Teri maa ki…" and similar gendered insults are more than merely vulgar expressions; they are cultural artifacts that expose how deeply society associates women with shame and vulnerability. These insults target women's relatives to wound male pride, reinforcing the idea that a woman's body is tied to honour and that its violation serves as a tool of humiliation. Such language normalizes the concept that women are extensions of male identity and that harming them is a legitimate form of retaliation or dominance.

Historically, sexual violence has been systematically deployed as a weapon during conflict and conquest. In war zones, rape has been used to terrorize populations, destabilize communities, and assert power. From the destruction of ancient cities to the horrors of concentration camps and modern genocides, sexual violence has served as a deliberate tactic of war. In some border regions, the preference for male children stems from the fear that daughters may be raped, bringing perceived "shame" upon the family. This tragic logic shows how the threat of sexual violence shapes reproductive choices and reinforces gender inequality. Even today, sexual violence remains a tool in mass displacement, ethnic cleansing, and political suppression, where women are seen as vulnerable, voiceless, and expendable targets.

In patriarchal societies, rape is sometimes rationalized as a way to "teach women a lesson," reflecting a belief that women must be controlled and that violence is a legitimate means of enforcing this control. These attitudes are reinforced by cultural narratives that blame victims, excuse perpetrators, and celebrate male dominance. Skewed sex ratios, often caused by female foeticide, create demographic imbalances that increase sexual frustration and aggression. A surplus of unmarried men, especially in economically deprived areas, heightens the risk of sexual violence, particularly when societal norms discourage emotional expression and healthy sexual development.

Economic desperation also fuels sexual aggression. Joblessness and poverty can intensify feelings of inadequacy and resentment. A young, unemployed man may feel emasculated by his inability to provide for or attract a partner. When faced with economically independent women, this frustration can turn to hostility, creating a dangerous mix of despair and sexual aggression that sometimes results in violence. Migration further complicates the issue, as men who leave their families for work often find themselves in emotionally and sexually isolated environments, where unchecked male peer groups can foster exploitation and abuse.

The Bilkis Bano case in India sadly exemplifies how societal attitudes, political influence, and institutional failure intersect in cases of sexual violence. The initial release and public celebration of the convicted rapists sent a devastating message, that justice can be negotiated, and women's suffering is secondary to political and social loyalties. Although the courts later reinstated their imprisonment, the damage was done, exposing a societal undercurrent where caste, creed, and political affiliation frequently override moral accountability.

This systemic failure extends to societal responses. The muted reaction to rape contrasts sharply with explosive outrage over perceived offenses against religious symbols, such as protests over "holy animals." This disparity reveals a troubling hierarchy of values where women's bodies are often treated as less sacred and their violation as less worthy of public outrage. Investigations into rape cases similarly gain traction mostly when they intersect with caste or communal tensions, highlighting systemic bias that leaves many survivors, especially those from marginalized communities, denied justice.

Sexual violence is therefore not an isolated or random occurrence. It is woven into the very fabric of society, perpetuated through language, historical patterns, economic structures, and institutional failures. Addressing it requires confronting not only individual perpetrators but also the systems that enable and excuse them. This demands a transformation of values, a redefinition of honour, and a commitment to justice that transcends caste, class, and creed. Only by un-weaving these threads of violence can society be re-stitched into one where dignity and safety are universal rights rather than privileges.

Chapter 32

Effects of Rape

Rape is a profoundly traumatic crime with consequences that ripple far beyond the moment of violation. Its impact touches every aspect of a survivor's life, physical, psychological, social, and financial, often leaving scars that endure for years, if not a lifetime. The physical toll can be immediate and severe. Survivors may suffer bruises, lacerations, broken bones, and internal injuries, including damage to the reproductive system. In the most tragic cases, the violence of the assault can result in death. Some survivors endure permanent disabilities, such as paralysis, loss of limbs, or vision impairment, especially when the assault involves extreme physical brutality. The risk of sexually transmitted infections is another grim reality. Survivors may contract HIV, chlamydia, gonorrhoea, or other STIs, adding a layer of medical and emotional distress to an already devastating experience. Chronic pain is also common, with some survivors developing long-term conditions that affect their mobility, comfort, and quality of life. Unwanted pregnancy resulting from rape presents its own set of challenges, forcing survivors to confront complex emotional, physical, and social decisions under immense psychological strain.

The psychological aftermath of rape is often even more enduring than the physical injuries. Many survivors develop post-traumatic stress disorder, characterized by intrusive memories, nightmares, severe anxiety, and avoidance of anything that reminds them of the trauma. Depression frequently follows, manifesting as deep sadness, hopelessness, and a loss of interest in life. Anxiety disorders, including generalized anxiety, panic attacks, and social anxiety, may emerge or intensify. In some cases, the trauma is so overwhelming that it triggers psychosis, leading to hallucinations or delusions. Survivors may also develop specific phobias related to the circumstances of the assault, such as fear of the dark or fear of strangers. Suicidal thoughts and attempts are tragically common, driven by the intense psychological pain and feelings of helplessness. Emotional numbing is another coping mechanism, where survivors detach from their feelings to avoid the pain, but this can lead to a sense of emptiness and disconnection from life. Trust becomes a fragile thing; survivors often struggle to form or maintain relationships, fearing vulnerability and betrayal. Many irrationally blame themselves for the assault, carrying guilt and shame that further erodes their self-worth.

The social consequences of rape extend the trauma into the survivor's community and relationships. Stigma remains a powerful force, leading to social isolation, discrimination, and judgment. In some cultures, survivors are segregated or shunned, even by their own families. Marriage prospects may be damaged, and existing relationships strained or broken. Families may fracture under the weight of the trauma, with conflict, separation, or divorce as possible outcomes. Survivors often withdraw from social life, losing the support networks that could aid their recovery. Victim blaming compounds the harm, as survivors are sometimes held responsible for the violence inflicted upon them. This toxic narrative not only deepens their trauma but also discourages others from coming forward. Media coverage can be another source of distress. Sensationalized or unethical reporting exposes survivors to public scrutiny and judgment, turning their pain into spectacle and further violating their dignity.

Rape does not only devastate individuals psychologically and physically; it imposes a significant economic burden on society. While the trauma experienced by survivors is irreplaceable, the ripple effects of each incident extend far beyond personal suffering. These cumulative costs, borne by individuals, families, communities, and the state, demand serious attention in any policy conversation on prevention and response. Survivors often require extensive medical and psychological care, including emergency treatment, long-term counselling, psychiatric support, and reproductive health services. These needs place a growing strain on public health infrastructure, especially in countries where access to trauma-informed care is limited. The financial cost of these services is substantial and recurring, affecting both public budgets and private households. In many cases, survivors are unable to return to work, either temporarily or permanently. The trauma, physical injuries, or social stigma can lead to a loss of productivity that impacts not only the individual but also their family and the broader economy. This is particularly significant in contexts where women are primary earners or contributors to household income. The loss of human capital is a silent but powerful consequence of sexual violence. The criminal justice system also bears a heavy cost. Investigating, prosecuting, and adjudicating rape cases requires substantial resources, police investigations, forensic testing, legal representation, court proceedings, and incarceration. These processes, while essential for justice, entail recurrent public expenditure. Governments that offer compensation to survivors add another layer of financial responsibility. While such compensation is ethically necessary, it becomes economically sustainable only when paired with effective prevention strategies. High-profile rape cases often expose systemic failures and spark public outrage. Mass mobilizations, protests, and civil disobedience, though vital expressions of resistance, can disrupt economic activity, damage infrastructure, and divert public resources. The cost of policing demonstrations, managing crowd control, and providing security to activists or survivors adds to the operational burden on the state. In India, the economic losses associated with each rape case, spanning healthcare, lost productivity, law enforcement, and public disruption, likely amount to several million rupees when accounted comprehensively. Ironically, this figure is often higher than the cost of implementing a nationwide anti-rape initiative. A strategically designed public health program could leverage existing infrastructure to deliver impactful results at a lower cost. Such a program might include specialized training for healthcare workers, ASHAs, police, and teachers; public awareness campaigns focused on consent and gender equity; incentives for private-sector participation in survivor support; and rapid-response forensic and trauma care units. The return on this investment is not only financial, it is social, cultural, and moral. When prevention is prioritized, trauma is reduced, justice becomes more attainable, and the socioeconomic fabric of society is strengthened.

PART V: SYSTEM CRITIQUES & FAILURES

Chapter 33

The Fallacy of Legalized Prostitution as Rape Prevention

The debate surrounding the legalization of prostitution often includes the contentious argument that such measures could lead to a reduction in sexual offenses, particularly rape. This assertion, while superficially appealing to some, is fundamentally flawed and rooted in a misunderstanding of the complex motivations behind sexual violence. By examining the nature of rape, the realities of the sex industry, and the inefficacy of addressing violent urges with transactional sex, it becomes clear that legalized prostitution is not a viable strategy for rape prevention.

Proponents of the theory that legalization reduces rape often suggest that providing a legal outlet for sexual urges will diminish the likelihood of individuals resorting to non-consensual acts. This perspective operates under the simplistic assumption that rape is primarily driven by unmet sexual desire. However, this analogy is akin to suggesting that readily available fast food will eradicate theft motivated by hunger, it misdiagnoses the underlying issue. Rape is not merely about sex; it is fundamentally an act of violence, power, control, and often, deep-seated misogyny and a lack of empathy. Equating the demand for transactional sex with the violent urge to dominate and violate another person is a dangerous oversimplification.

The core distinction between prostitution and rape lies in the presence or absence of consent. Prostitution, in its idealized form, involves a transaction where sexual services are exchanged willingly for compensation. Rape, conversely, is the non-consensual penetration of another person, a violent violation of bodily autonomy and fundamental human rights. To suggest that the availability of consensual sexual acts would deter non-consensual ones ignores the perpetrator's intent. A rapist seeks to exert power, inflict harm, and control their victim, objectives entirely separate from the acquisition of sexual release through a paid transaction.

Empirical evidence and the lived experiences of sex workers consistently demonstrate their heightened vulnerability to violence, including rape. Legalization, while potentially offering some regulatory frameworks, does not inherently eliminate the power imbalances and exploitative environments that can prevail within the sex industry. Pimps, clients, and other actors can still perpetrate violence against sex workers, often with impunity. To argue that making prostitution legal would reduce rape while simultaneously acknowledging the continued risk of sexual violence against those within the industry is a profound contradiction. It suggests a willingness to sacrifice the safety and well-being of one group to potentially benefit another, based on a flawed premise.

Consider several scenarios that further illustrate the ineffectiveness of legalized prostitution in preventing rape. Individuals with a sexual attraction to children are driven by a specific paraphilia that involves minors. Legalized adult prostitution would be entirely irrelevant to their desires and behaviours. Perpetrators who intend to "teach a woman a lesson" through rape are motivated by anger, resentment, and a desire for retribution. Paying for sex would not fulfil this objective of inflicting emotional and physical trauma on a specific individual. Acquaintance and date rape often occur within existing social relationships and are driven by a sense of entitlement, misinterpretation of cues, or a disregard for consent. The availability of prostitutes has no bearing on these dynamics. Gang rape is frequently about asserting dominance, male bonding through violence, and the degradation of the victim. The idea that a group of individuals intending to commit such an act would instead visit a brothel for a gang rape service is illogical and unsupported by any understanding of the motivations behind this heinous crime. Sexual assaults that occur in specific contexts, such as a teacher molesting a student or friends raping someone on a picnic, are driven by power dynamics within those specific situations and the perpetrator's individual motivations. The existence of legal prostitution elsewhere would not prevent these acts.

The historical debate surrounding prostitution as the "oldest profession" is largely irrelevant to the discussion of rape prevention. Whether or not sex work has ancient roots does not lend any credence to the argument that its legalization would impact sexual violence. This is a semantic distraction from the core issue of understanding the motivations behind rape.

Legalized prostitution, while worthy of discussion in terms of labour rights, health regulation, and social policy, should not be misrepresented as a solution to sexual violence. The motivations behind rape are complex, rooted in power, control, and systemic inequality. Addressing these requires a multifaceted approach, education, accountability, cultural change, not the commodification of consent.

Chapter 34

The Unprotected: Victim Safety in the Bail System

The scales of justice are famously depicted as balanced, symbolizing fairness and impartiality. Yet, for countless victims of crime, particularly in the harrowing period before a verdict is reached, these scales often feel profoundly skewed, heavy with anxiety, fear, and a chilling sense of exposure. While the legal system grapples with the fundamental principles of presumed innocence and the right to liberty, an unspoken terror can loom for those who have suffered at the hands of alleged perpetrators: the terrifying reality that the very individuals accused of harming them might walk free, even if temporarily, and pose a renewed threat.

Let's discuss the disturbing vulnerabilities faced by victims and their families when alleged perpetrators are granted bail. It examines the critical gaps in oversight, the urgent need for robust protections, and the ethical dilemmas inherent in balancing the rights of the accused with the paramount need for public and victim safety.

Perhaps the most visceral and agonizing fear for a victim is the prospect of their alleged attacker returning to their lives, sometimes with devastating consequences. We hear the grim reports, sometimes from our own communities: "Under-trials have killed their victims' parents." "Many of the under-trials have attacked the victim, including their families; sometimes they have killed the victim's relatives after securing a bail." These aren't isolated incidents; they are stark reminders of a systemic failure, where the very mechanisms designed to ensure justice inadvertently expose the most vulnerable to further harm. The purpose of bail, in its purest form, is to allow an individual accused of a crime to remain free until their trial, provided they pose no flight risk, no threat to evidence or witnesses, and critically, no danger to the community or specific individuals. Yet, when these conditions are misjudged or inadequately enforced, the system fractures. The horrifying reality of a victim or their family facing retribution, intimidation, or even further violence from an individual awaiting trial is a profound betrayal of the social contract. It transforms the waiting period for justice into a gauntlet of terror.

Compounding this fear is the perceived lack of a robust "tool or monitoring system" for repeat offenders. Imagine the scenario: an individual with a documented history of violence, or previous brushes with the law, is released on bail. Without stringent oversight, electronic monitoring, or consistent check-ins, the risk they pose can escalate from theoretical to terrifyingly real. The concerns extend beyond new crimes; they encompass the potential for intimidation, tampering with evidence, or threats against those brave enough to testify. The current landscape, as perceived by many, often lacks adequate mechanisms to track, restrain, or even adequately assess the ongoing threat posed by such individuals. This gap creates a dangerous void where recidivism can flourish, and victims are left feeling abandoned and unprotected by the very institutions meant to safeguard them.

The urgent need for reform is clear, driven by the real-world experiences of victims. The call for "strict rules to be formulated for under-trials" is not merely punitive; it's a plea for fundamental safety. This encompasses a range of potential interventions. The pursuit of justice also hinges on evidence, and often, the most compelling evidence comes from those who witnessed the crime. Yet, "strict witness protection programmes" are often underdeveloped, underfunded, or simply non-existent in many jurisdictions. If a witness fears reprisal from an under-trial out on bail, their willingness to testify evaporates. This can lead to cases collapsing, perpetrators walking free, and a cycle of impunity that further erodes public trust. A truly effective justice system must ensure that those who come forward to aid in the pursuit of truth can do so without risking their lives or the safety of their loved ones.

The concerns articulated by those most affected by crime are specific and resolute. There are powerful demands for "methods to restrain or protect the victim or not to provide bail to any perpetrator till the conviction happens." This is a direct appeal for proactive and absolute victim protection, challenging the traditional understanding of pre-trial liberty for certain categories of offenders. A particularly strong sentiment calls for "no bail or parole rules for rape perpetrators." This powerful demand reflects the unique trauma and profound violation inherent in sexual assault. The very thought of a perpetrator of such a crime being free, even on conditional bail, before conviction, is an unbearable burden for victims and a stark symbol of a system perceived as failing to protect them. The argument here transcends legal nuance; it's a moral imperative rooted in the horrific nature of the crime and the need to prevent any further harm or intimidation. In extreme cases, where threats remain even after a conviction, the idea of an "identity change for victim till once the justice is served and criminal is punished" highlights the profound and lasting fear some victims endure.

The challenge for legal systems globally is immense: how to uphold the foundational principles of justice while simultaneously providing an unshakeable shield of protection for victims. This requires not just legislative reform, but a profound cultural shift within the justice system itself – one that places the safety and well-being of victims at the forefront, not as an afterthought. The voices of those who have faced the "under-trial labyrinth" are a poignant and powerful call to action. Their experiences illuminate the unseen shadows where fear lingers, and where the promise of justice feels distant. Only by acknowledging these vulnerabilities and actively working to address them can we hope to build a system that truly serves all its citizens, and where the scales of justice are not just balanced in theory, but in the lived reality of every individual.

Chapter 35

The Shadow of Accusation

Justice rests on a principle as fragile as it is vital: that truth must guide judgment. In the struggle against sexual violence, where the stakes are human dignity and safety, this principle is often stretched to its limits. In recent times, the spectre of false allegations of rape and sexual harassment has become an unsettling reality, casting a long shadow over the lives it touches. For those falsely accused, the descent into the machinery of law often brings devastation far beyond the courtroom. Reputations are destroyed, livelihoods lost, families fractured, and in the most tragic instances, despair drives individuals to irreversible acts. Sometimes what begins with an accusation concludes not in justice but in retaliation, as a life stripped of dignity grasps for some semblance of control. In such moments, the delicate balance of justice itself teeters dangerously, torn between the need to protect genuine survivors and the responsibility to shield the innocent from wrongful ruin.

Much of this unease arises from the shifting patterns of modern relationships and the fragile boundaries between intimacy, trust, and betrayal. Increasingly, couples cohabit outside of marriage, their lives entangled in shared experiences and physical closeness. Yet when affection wanes and separation looms, the line between a broken heart and a criminal allegation can blur with alarming ease. A quarrel, a misunderstanding, or even the bitterness of rejection can suddenly be reframed as assault, pulling consensual encounters into the language of coercion. Courts confronted with such cases face terrain that is not only legally complex but emotionally charged, demanding a level of discernment and sensitivity that cannot be reduced to blunt categories of guilt and innocence.

There is an added dimension to this imbalance. In some cases, men who have invested emotionally and financially in a relationship find themselves devastated when the promise of marriage is withdrawn. Their sense of betrayal, deepened by financial loss and humiliation, seems to fall outside the scope of law, leaving them with no avenue of redress. Legal systems, shaped primarily to provide protection for women, often appear blind to the emotional exploitation men may also face in intimate partnerships. Even raising such questions is fraught with sensitivity, for it must never be used to dilute the urgent need for protecting women from violence. Yet without honest engagement with imbalance, the promise of equal justice feels partial and unfulfilled.

Stories drawn from real life illustrate the fragile and sometimes tragic collisions between intimacy and law. Consider the case of a high school girl who met secretly with a boy from her neighbourhood. Their encounters were consensual, shaped by youthful vulnerability and the curiosity of first intimacy. Such meetings remained hidden until fate betrayed their secrecy. Upon being caught by her mother, fear seized the girl so intensely that she fabricated a tale of abduction and rape to shield herself from parental fury. The alarmed mother rushed to the police, and within hours, official action was underway. Yet when confronted under investigation, the girl broke down and admitted to the consensual truth. Instead of correcting course and questioning the misuse of serious charges, the police redirected their punitive hand toward the boy, invoking the stringent provisions of the POCSO Act. What was overlooked was the essential distinction between a fabricated fear-driven narrative and an actual crime of violence. The law, in its blunt severity, consumed not only the truth of the situation but also a boy whose agency was little greater than the girl's.

Such cases signal the urgent need for re-examining the very definition of rape in legal contexts, especially as society grapples with changing social norms. Perhaps the law must hold to a stricter foundation: that rape constitutes the absence of consent and the presence of force. Without clear evidence of refusal and coercion, criminalizing consensual intimacy that later turns regretted or socially condemned risks burdening the justice system with cases rooted in misunderstanding rather than actual violence. Narrowing the definition to reflect the essence of non-consent could help sift genuine offenses from those born of social shame, emotional fallout, or family pressure.

The complexities deepen when we consider the Protection of Children from Sexual Offences Act. Enacted with noble intent, POCSO has given many minors the shield they long needed against predators. Yet in practice it sometimes functions as a double-edged sword. In communities where child marriage persists as an entrenched social practice, young men, themselves little more than boys, are imprisoned for acts that flow not from calculated predation but from traditions imposed by elders.

Instead of targeting the orchestrators such as parents, relatives, community figures, the law falls heaviest on those who are equally vulnerable, often themselves denied choice or agency in matters of marriage and intimacy. The punishment becomes misdirected, undermining the very goal of breaking a harmful tradition.

Elopement cases tell a similar tale of imbalance. When young lovers choose to run away, even at the girl's urging or initiative, it is invariably the boy who confronts the iron consequences of the law. The girl is often portrayed as victimized, absolved of will or responsibility, while the boy alone bears the stigma of criminality. This not only erases the girl's agency but also reinforces the troubling assumption that young women cannot be capable of informed choice, even while men of equal age are expected to bear its weight with the burden of law.

Taken together, these overlapping realities reveal a legal and enforcement system struggling to keep pace with evolving interpersonal dynamics and shifting social contexts. At one extreme lies the undeniable need to protect women and children from genuine violence, coercion, and systemic exploitation. At the other lies the risk of weaponizing laws, where accusations, misunderstandings, or entrenched cultural norms are transformed into devastating criminal charges. The outcome in either case is often injustice, sometimes for survivors denied swift resolution, at other times for the innocent whose lives are eroded by falsehood.

The reluctance in certain jurisdictions to even lodge a First Information Report further underscores systemic inconsistencies, for it exposes how discretion is wielded between under-enforcement in some cases and overcriminalization in others. This duality erodes faith in the fairness of institutions. A comprehensive re-evaluation of both substantive law and enforcement practices is no longer merely desirable but essential. Justice cannot be served when protection for one is built upon the ruin of another. Instead, reform must strive to draw careful lines: defending the vulnerable, holding perpetrators accountable, yet ensuring that intimacy, youthful mistakes, or failed relationships are not mechanistically conflated with rape or reprehensible violence. Only then will the law recover its balance, between compassion and fairness, vigilance and prudence, and serve justice without prejudice.

Chapter 36

The Siren Song and the Unintended Curriculum

Exposure and influence have become inseparable forces in the digital era. Children are no longer guarded by distance from what was once considered adult knowledge; a passing reference, a stray remark, is enough to open new doors of discovery. The question we face is not whether they will encounter such ideas, but whether we, as a society, exercise the foresight to guide them responsibly. When influence is mishandled, particularly around issues of sexuality, curiosity is fuelled rather than restrained, revealing the urgent need to rethink who we hold up as figures of authority and what narratives they offer to the young.

Consider an unsettling anecdote. A performer from the adult industry, attempting what might have been intended as a light-hearted act of outreach, once advised school children not to watch "Naughty America" but to watch "Captain America." The advice, however flippant, carried consequences that were immediately counterproductive. For children previously unaware of the term, a new and forbidden frontier was suddenly unveiled. Curiosity, one of the most powerful impulses of human psychology, was sparked, and it is not difficult to imagine how easily it might lead them toward searching for exactly what the speaker had so casually mentioned. What was framed as subtle guidance turned instead into an inadvertent invitation, exposing how fragile the line has become between adult content and mainstream exposure, particularly in a world where access to instant information and pornographic material is just a tap away. This example underscores not only a lack of foresight but also a disconcerting underestimation of the psychological power of suggestion. Allowing individuals whose professional identities are bound to explicit content to lecture children, however noble their intent, reflects a worrying lapse of common sense about role models and the formative influence of public figures on young impressionable minds. The argument here is not about judging private choices made by adults, but about recognizing influence as a form of power and the risks attached when it is exercised without responsibility.

Part of the danger stems from the ways in which the lives of adult performers are framed and consumed by the public. Documentaries, interviews, and social media often present what appears to be a flamboyant lifestyle: wealth, glamour, confidence, independence, and the allure of unrestricted freedom. Particularly for the young, these constructed images can be intoxicating. Teenage girls may aspire to such

paths, seeing in them a form of agency or liberation. Yet what is rarely acknowledged in these glossy depictions is the darker underbelly of the industry. Beneath the glamorized narrative lies an often-devastating reality marked by relentless risks and unspoken suffering.

Health hazards are among the most visible yet underreported aspects. High rates of sexually transmitted diseases, including HIV, remain a constant threat in the industry, where frequent exposure and unequal power dynamics compromise safety practices. Alongside physical risk runs an even more pervasive psychological toll. Many performers struggle with depression, anxiety, and post-traumatic stress. For some, substance use becomes a way of numbing the cycle of performance and alienation; for others, loneliness and emotional detachment corrode attempts to reintegrate into "ordinary" life. Stories of suicide among both current and former performers are tragic reminders of the despair and exhaustion that often hide behind curated appearances. Even the boundary around consent, outwardly treated as contractual and voluntary, is frequently undermined by coercion, manipulation, or economic exploitation, blurring the difference between choice and survival.

What emerges, then, is a deliberately imbalanced narrative. The industry and an enabling media ecosystem highlight only the glamour, fame, money, visibility, while pushing aside the anguish, the exploitation, the health risks, and the dislocation that characterize too many experiences within it. Vulnerable youth are thus presented with a one-sided illusion, their aspirations shaped by fantasy while the costs remain concealed. The ethical burden of this is immense, demanding far greater candour in how this world is portrayed and a deeper reckoning with the consequences of presenting such pathways as enticing, "empowered" careers without reference to the harm that so often follows.

This conversation grows even more pressing when juxtaposed with the way society treats survivors of sexual violence. Here, the starkness of the double standard becomes unbearable. Those who commit rape are often dealt with under the law and may eventually walk free after serving their sentences, reintegrating into society with striking ease. An individual who has committed such a crime may find work, marry, raise children, and reestablish himself within a community that too readily forgets or overlooks what he has done. By contrast, the woman he has harmed faces a lifelong sentence far beyond the legal judgment. She suffers stigma that permeates every aspect of her existence: her dignity is questioned, her marriage prospects severely diminished, and her social acceptance conditioned by whispers and prejudice. She is marked, not by her own act but by one committed upon her, and she is forced to relive it in the way society sees and treats her.

The paradox deepens when public attitudes toward adult entertainment are considered. Performers from the pornographic industry, despite their careers being defined by explicit sex on camera, are often embraced as celebrities. They appear on talk shows, write memoirs, raise children openly, and cultivate large followings on social media. In many circles, they are admired for their candidness, treated as figures of resilience or even glamour. Their lives, despite being organized around commodified intimacy, often command respect. But when the lens shifts to a rape survivor, someone who never consented, who endured an assault against her will, society recoils. Rather than acceptance, it heaps shame. Rather than restoring dignity, it strips it further. Rather than offering reintegration, it enforces exclusion.

This contradiction is more than hypocrisy; it reveals a devastating cultural flaw. We celebrate individuals whose fame emerges from commercial sex work, yet condemn survivors whose only "act" was to endure trauma forced upon them. In doing so, we invert morality: choosing to embrace glamourized commodification yet choosing to ostracize a victim of brutal violation. The asymmetry is painful, but perhaps it also provides clarity. If society is capable of extending acceptance to those who trade in explicit entertainment, it is entirely within its power to extend dignity to those who have endured violence. If anything, survivors deserve far more compassion, support, and opportunities for renewal than those whose lives are built upon voluntary adult performance.

The question remains: if society can normalize, even celebrate, one form of sexual life, why does it continue to shun women who are survivors of sexual harm? Until this inversion is reconciled, until survivors are seen not with suspicion but with solidarity, and until portrayal of adult industries becomes more honest and grounded, we risk perpetuating a cultural landscape where stigma is more enduring than crime, and where trauma endures not for what was done, but for how society chooses to remember it.

This comparison compels us to ask: Do porn performers or the platforms that host their content bear any moral responsibility for the broader societal consequences of sexual violence? While their content is consensual and legal among adults, the pervasive normalization of various sexual scenarios and explicit imagery may inadvertently influence public attitudes, potentially desensitizing viewers to the true gravity of non-consensual sexual acts. Yet, there is remarkably little public discourse on the accountability or ethical boundaries of an industry that, whether directly or indirectly, contributes to the sexual landscape of society.

The question of "who is taking moral responsibility" extends beyond the performers and the immediate production companies. It encompasses the web of websites, advertisers, payment processors, and, crucially, the consumers themselves. Producers and distributors must consider their moral obligation to ensure performer well-being and portray reality accurately. Website operators and platforms, as primary gatekeepers, have a moral duty to verify age and genuine consent, balancing freedom of expression with preventing harm. And for consumers, the demand drives the supply; the act of consuming pornography, especially content known or suspected to be exploitative, carries **moral weight**, creating a **shared responsibility** in its perpetuation.

Perhaps the most heartbreaking manifestation of this societal hypocrisy lies in the intimate sphere: Can society truly accept a rape survivor as a daughter-in-law or wife? This question exposes deep-rooted prejudices that continue to plague many communities. Survivors are all too often deemed 'impure,' 'damaged,' or somehow 'unfit' for marriage, despite being the innocent victims of a heinous crime. The reluctance to embrace them fully into familial and marital roles reflects a profound failure of empathy, a primitive assigning of blame to the victim, and an urgent need for fundamental **cultural transformation**.

The current state is untenable. Survivors deserve dignity, compassion, and the fundamental right to pursue a normal, fulfilling life, unburdened by a crime committed against them. The immense burden of shame must be definitively and unequivocally shifted from the victim to the perpetrator, where it rightfully belongs. Society must evolve to actively support healing, facilitate reintegration, and champion the empowerment of survivors. This critical evolution necessitates a multifaceted approach, including robust **public education** campaigns to dismantle harmful myths, comprehensive **legal reforms** that prioritize victim rights, and, most importantly, a collective, unwavering commitment from every member of society to dismantling the deeply ingrained stigma that continues to haunt the innocent. Only then can we truly claim to be a just and empathetic society.

Chapter 37

The Eroticization of the Everyday and the Erosion of Boundaries

In contemporary society, the term "sexy" has undergone a notable transformation, from a once-weighted descriptor to a casual, even celebratory label. Within mainstream Indian media, particularly Bollywood, its overuse has rendered it nearly mundane. Actresses are openly addressed as "sexy" at award functions, often in the presence of their families, and this label is frequently received with pride. While such usage may appear harmless, its normalization sets a precarious precedent. In a world without constant security or protective oversight, the public's internalized association between being "sexy" and being desirable can increase vulnerability, especially for women and girls.

This phenomenon reflects a broader societal trend: a gradual yet consistent erosion of moral and cultural boundaries in the quest to emulate global (often Western) entertainment norms. In educational settings, cultural programs increasingly favour dances to popular film music over indigenous traditions, folk songs, classical pieces, and regional stories once central to identity formation. It is not uncommon to see toddlers and young children performing choreographed routines to sexually suggestive songs, dressed in revealing costumes, cheered on by audiences unaware, or unbothered, by the implications.

Meanwhile, reality television, with its wide reach and influence, contributes to a desensitization of sexual innuendo through double-entendre humour and objectifying commentary. Even authority figures, judges, hosts, mentors, are not immune from this trend, as their public personas are often crafted to exude charisma that leans on overt sexual appeal. Within this matrix of media, education, and entertainment, "being forward" is frequently confused with being sexually provocative.

Young minds absorb far more than we acknowledge. When constant messaging equates worth with a "sexy voice," "sexy body," or "sexy appearance," it reshapes children's understanding of self-worth, relationships, and boundaries. Over time, this pervasive messaging blurs the line between appreciation and objectification, potentially fostering attitudes that enable or excuse predatory behaviour.

The result is a society where sexual aggressiveness becomes not only normalized but, in some cases, admired or mistaken for confidence. The internalization of such values at a young age has profound implications for both gender dynamics and vulnerability to exploitation.

Unfortunately, societal erosion is compounded by institutional failure. It is a matter of national shame that many victims of sexual violence are mistreated by those tasked with their protection. Police response, particularly in the absence of public pressure or media intervention, is often lethargic or dismissive. Investigations may be delayed or denied until politicians or journalists intervene. This reactive posture reflects not only a lack of sensitivity but also a failure of systemic accountability.

Moreover, the current legal and media ecosystem operates largely without input from mental health professionals. While police and lawyers handle procedural matters and the media amplifies cases, often with sensationalism, psychological expertise is glaringly absent from the investigation process. There is no structured inclusion of psychologists in the study of victims or perpetrators, leaving critical insights unexplored.

In India, most psychological investigations into the minds of rapists are carried out informally, by students, volunteers, or researchers working pro bono. As a result, we lack a comprehensive national database of psychological profiles, behavioural patterns, or risk indicators specific to our cultural and socio-economic landscape. This knowledge gap hinders the development of locally relevant educational materials and prevention strategies.

In contrast, many nations have invested heavily in evidence-based strategies to understand and prevent sexual violence. Researchers like Dr. Neil Malamuth and Dr. Sharon Smythyman have contributed foundational work that Indian policymakers and academic institutions can learn from. Dr. Malamuth's "Confluence Model of Sexual Aggression" explores how hostile masculinity and an impersonal approach to sex intersect to increase the likelihood of sexual aggression. Dr. Smythyman's work on "undetected rapists", based on anonymous interviews, uncovers how many perpetrators rationalize their actions, often expressing little guilt. This insight has proved invaluable for risk assessment and early intervention. The Rape Myth Acceptance Scale (RMAS) and studies on Workplace Gendered Rape and Assault (WGRA) offer quantifiable tools to assess cultural beliefs and institutional vulnerabilities.

These are not merely academic pursuits. They are practical frameworks with real-world implications, allowing for predictive modelling, prevention education, and risk-reduction strategies. India must move beyond viewing rape solely as a legal or moral failing, it must treat it as a public health crisis informed by interdisciplinary expertise.

The eroticization of the everyday is not an inevitable byproduct of modernity, it is a cultural choice. The values we embed in entertainment, education, and public discourse shape future generations' understanding of gender, consent, and sexuality. If we continue to conflate empowerment with hyper sexualization, and confidence with objectification, we risk cultivating a society that normalizes the very violence we seek to eradicate.

What is urgently needed is a recalibration of values across every social institution. This means embedding cultural sensitivity and age-appropriate norms into school curriculums, regulating media representations of sexuality, especially involving minors, institutionalizing psychological profiling of offenders within legal investigations, training police and educators in trauma-informed approaches, and above all, investing in original research and psychological infrastructure to generate India-specific strategies for prevention and support.

Sexual violence does not arise in a vacuum, it festers in the grey zones where boundaries erode and accountability falters. The time has come to redraw those boundaries and reclaim the dignity of the everyday.

PART VI: SOLUTION FRAMEWORKS

Chapter 38

Rapist is Killed, Long Live the Crime

The immediate assassination of a criminal, while perhaps offering a visceral sense of justice or closure, ultimately truncates the potential for deeper understanding and prevention of the crime itself. While the legal system may continue its course, the summary execution of a perpetrator, especially one as reviled as a rapist, effectively silences a potential source of invaluable insight into the genesis of such heinous acts.

To truly address the pervasive issue of sexual violence, a comprehensive understanding of the criminal mind is paramount. This requires a thorough investigation into the individual's antecedents: the "why" and "how" behind their actions. Exploring their psychology, family history, upbringing, and the specific situations that may have contributed to their path is crucial. Such inquiries could yield significant insights into the complex interplay of factors that culminate in the commission of rape.

Like many individuals convicted of violent crimes, rapists often develop their own intricate systems of justification, sometimes even glorifying their acts in their own minds. Unravelling the cognitive distortions and moral disengagement mechanisms that allow them to rationalize their behaviour is essential to understanding the psychology of a rapist. How does an otherwise seemingly "normal" boy transition into someone capable of such profound violation? What specific developmental trajectories, traumas, or learned behaviours contribute to this transformation?

The information gleaned from in-depth studies and interviews with convicted rapists could be instrumental in developing crucial tools for crime prevention. This might include the creation of risk assessment scores to predict potential offenders or the development of targeted interventions to reduce the likelihood of future crimes. The very reasons behind the rampant prevalence of rape may lie, in part, within our current approaches to understanding and handling perpetrators.

Research and interviews conducted with convicts in cases like the Nirbhaya case and within the American prison system have already yielded substantial information. This wealth of data holds the potential to be synthesized into invaluable resources for psychology students, police officers, and forensic experts alike, offering a deeper understanding of the criminal mind and potentially paving the way for more effective strategies in combating sexual violence. The silencing of a criminal, however reprehensible their acts, closes a door to potential knowledge that could ultimately contribute to a safer society.

Chapter 39

Reclaiming Safety, Treating Sexual Violence as a Public Health Emergency

There are crises that confront a nation with sudden force, demanding attention through their sheer immediacy, and there are others that seep quietly into daily life until they become part of the air we breathe. Sexual violence belongs to the latter category, a silent epidemic that corrodes trust, safety, and dignity at every level of society. It does not erupt like a natural disaster, nor does it announce itself like an outbreak of disease. Instead, it persists with a chilling regularity, each incident both familiar and devastating, reminding us that the threat is not exceptional but embedded in the everyday.

The headlines are relentless, each one another reminder of a life irrevocably altered, another story of violence carried into the public gaze and then allowed to fade. The scale of sexual violence in our society is no longer shocking; it is numbing. Thousands of women endure the trauma of rape each day, a reality so devastating and persistent that it repeats itself across news cycles until it becomes background noise. Yet beneath this churn of media and public outrage lies a harsher truth: sexual violence is not only a profound human tragedy but a national emergency left unaddressed at its roots.

For decades the response has been tethered to the criminal justice system, summoned only after the harm is done. Law enforcement and legal institutions, though vital to accountability, cannot undo trauma nor intercept it before it unfolds. These systems are designed to respond to a crime, not to prevent it, and their failure to curb the overwhelming tide signals not a lapse in enforcement but a fundamental shortcoming in approach. What if we chose to treat sexual violence not merely as a moral failure or a criminal act but as a public health emergency, the way we do with pandemics or rising chronic diseases? Such a shift would mean moving away from a reactive, punitive model toward one centred on prevention, an approach situated at the population level where society itself is examined for its risks, its weaknesses, and its capacity to change.

In this vision, a central role emerges for the public health psychologist: a professional who understands both the intricacies of individual trauma and the broader social conditions that enable harm. Positioned outside the corridor of the courtroom or the desk of a police station, this figure steps in before violence occurs. Prevention becomes the true site of intervention. Public health as a discipline excels in diagnosing the upstream causes of crises, and applying this lens to sexual violence allows us to map the social, psychological, and cultural risk factors that fuel harm. Power imbalances, histories of unaddressed childhood trauma, distorted notions of masculinity, economic marginalization, and a culture that trivializes coercion are not isolated oddities; they are predictable breeding grounds for violence. Treating sexual assault as an outcome of untreated social disease means we can begin to chart pathways toward prevention, rather than perpetually managing its aftermath.

Through data-driven profiling, behavioural sciences, and community engagement, public health psychologists can identify individuals and environments at elevated risk, much like we screen populations for heart disease or diabetes. Emotional volatility, harmful attitudes toward gender, or environments that normalize aggression can all serve as markers for early, meaningful intervention. Once identified, these risks can be addressed through therapeutic support, educational reorientation about masculinity, and mentorship programs that steer individuals toward healthier models of relating. Early intervention of this kind has the power not only to halt a trajectory of potential harm but also to realign a life before it takes a destructive turn.

Prevention cannot, however, remain confined to private therapy rooms. Its deepest strength lies in community action, where collective values and daily practices are shaped. Public health professionals, trained to build trust and adapt interventions to specific contexts, can work with schools, workplaces, and local leaders to create campaigns that dismantle myths about rape, promote consent, and advocate for respectful relationships. What emerges is not just education but a deliberate re-engineering of cultural norms so that behaviours that once passed unchallenged are no longer tolerated.

The economic case for such an approach is equally compelling. The costs associated with rape, from healthcare and lost productivity to public unrest and compensation, accumulate into immense societal losses each year. By contrast, investing in a robust public health strategy aimed at prevention could mean spending far less while achieving far more. India in particular has the potential to adapt its existing health infrastructure, community health workers, local clinics, and private medical networks, toward this preventative framework. With the right training, alignment, and specialized services, not only could prevention and reporting improve, but survivor care and community resilience could be strengthened in ways that profoundly transform daily life.

Sexual violence is not inevitable. It is the outcome of silence, inequality, warped cultural assumptions, and systemic neglect. Like any public health crisis, it can be addressed when society treats it with urgency, seriousness, and foresight. Reclaiming safety means reclaiming agency, not only from perpetrators but also from outdated systems that rely exclusively on punishment after the fact. This is the moment to reimagine the struggle, not through greater force but through greater clarity of vision, not confined to courtrooms but wide open in classrooms, clinics, and community spaces.

To operationalize this model, society must engage at the stage before crimes occur. Professionals trained in behavioural sciences can identify at-risk youth and guide them toward self-regulation and respect, integrate ethics and consent education into school curricula, and foster community-led programs that emphasize resilience and equality. Such measures prevent harm but also promote emotional health, gender equity, and social trust, reinforcing the collective fabric against violence. A public health lens further ensures that care does not end once immediate wounds are addressed. Survivors can be supported through trauma-informed services, peer networks, and integrated pathways that connect healthcare, legal aid, and livelihood opportunities. Those at risk of committing violence can also be met with interventions that redirect destructive impulses before they calcify into crime.

Equally important is policy advocacy, for systemic change cannot rest on isolated fieldwork alone. Public health professionals can leverage evidence and community insights to shape school regulations, workplace safeguards, and healthcare policies that actively prevent harassment and assault. They can push for survivor-centred legislation, adequate funding, transparency, and cross-sector collaboration, all of which are crucial for long-term reform. Implementing such a framework will not be without challenges. Ethical vigilance is essential in protecting privacy, avoiding stigmatization, and managing sensitive risk assessments. Infrastructure investments, specialized training, and sustained coordination across health, education, justice, and social sectors will all be required.

More than anything, however, what is needed is a conceptual shift. Sexual violence is not solely an act of individual criminality. It is a symptom of deeper social illness, one whose spread can be slowed and even reversed through collective will and public health strategies. The choice before us is whether to remain numbed by relentless headlines or to act with vision, investing in prevention that heals, protects, and transforms.

What we face is not beyond repair, but repair will demand a readiness to think differently about violence itself. By treating it as a public health emergency, we finally create the chance to stem its tide at its source and to give future generations the safety and dignity they deserve.

Chapter 40

The Shadow of Perversion, Parental Roles, Paedophilia, and Child Protection

Sexual violence against children represents one of the most grotesque and insidious forms of human behaviour. It's devastating impact on victims and society warrants a direct and unflinching examination, not only of the crimes themselves but also of the cultural, psychological, and parental structures that permit such abuse to persist.

A jarring example of this perversion recently surfaced in the public sphere: following a high-stakes cricket match, a disheartened fan took to social media to issue a vile threat of sexual violence, not against an opposing player, but against the player's daughter, a toddler. This abhorrent act, though rooted in irrational rage, reveals a deeper societal sickness: the objectification and targeting of children as extensions of male vengeance, power, and fantasy.

Children are especially vulnerable due to their emotional

dependency, limited understanding of social cues, and trust in adults. Simple lures, like a chocolate, a toy, or attention, can render them defenceless in the hands of a predator. Tragically, spaces meant to foster safety and learning, schools, nurseries, homes, are increasingly revealed as sites where abuse occurs, often at the hands of those charged with protection and care.

Well-meaning educational efforts such as "good touch, bad touch" programs, while valuable, have proven insufficient on their own. Without structural and familial safeguards, such lessons are rarely enough to prevent coercion or to equip children to speak out against abuse. Moreover, these efforts often place the onus of detection on the child, rather than addressing the conditions that allow abuse to occur in the first place.

One of the most chilling aspects of child sexual abuse is the proximity of the perpetrator. A majority of reported cases involve someone known to the child, often a relative, neighbour, or family friend. These relationships of trust and familiarity not only make children more accessible but also more silenced, especially when the abuse is cloaked in fear, confusion, or manipulation.

Even more horrifying is the trajectory some of these crimes take. A child's inability to remain silent or comply, traits often misread as "risk" factors, may lead perpetrators to resort to murder in an effort to cover their crimes. Unlike adults, whose silence may be a survival strategy, a child's instinct is to cry out, often triggering violent escalation.

This dynamic exposes a dual tragedy: a failure of protection and a failure of prevention.

A deeper layer of complexity arises when considering the family environment. While it is true that a child's innocence can make them vulnerable, it is equally true that parental negligence, whether intentional or unintentional, plays a substantial role in enabling access to potential abusers. Leaving children unsupervised, normalizing secrecy within families, or ignoring emotional distress all create openings for exploitation.

Even more sobering is the data suggesting that many adult sexual offenders have their own histories of childhood abuse. This underscores the intergenerational nature of trauma, in which unresolved suffering and dysfunctional family systems contribute to cycles of violence.

To break these cycles, parental education must be seen not as a luxury but as a public health imperative. Parents must be equipped not only to recognize signs of abuse but to raise children in emotionally healthy, respectful, and communicative environments. This includes understanding the signs of grooming and boundary violations, the importance of open dialogue about body autonomy, the risks of permissive trust extended to friends, relatives, or authority figures, and the long-term emotional consequences of both abuse and silence.

Such education should not be reactive. Instead, it must be integrated into key transitional moments, such as during marriage registration, childbirth preparation, or early parenting programs. Pre-marriage counselling, for instance, offers a strategic platform to introduce critical discussions around healthy relationships, consent, and child protection. In a society where many couples receive no formal sexual education, this intervention could lay the groundwork for more informed, conscious parenting and safer domestic environments.

In many cultural contexts, significant attention is paid to ceremonial aspects of marriage, rituals, festivities, and aesthetics, while foundational conversations about family dynamics, parenting, and protection are entirely absent. This is a missed opportunity. Imagine if, instead of only focusing on wedding rituals, couples received guided discussions on emotional bonding and communication, safe and respectful intimacy, parenting roles and shared responsibilities, preventing domestic and sexual violence, and building protective environments for future children.

This kind of early, structured dialogue has the potential to shift mindsets before harmful patterns take root. It reframes marriage and family life as conscious commitments to safety, trust, and mutual respect.

Children cannot be tasked with their own protection. That responsibility falls squarely on adults, and by extension, society. To confront the horror of child sexual abuse, we must treat it not only as a criminal issue but as a cultural and parental failure that requires systemic correction. Protecting children means educating parents. Preventing abuse means confronting the taboo. Healing generations means stopping cycles before they start. If we truly wish to dismantle the shadow of perversion that looms over our children, we must begin not in the courtroom, but in the home, the classroom, and the counselling room, where beliefs are formed, where behaviours are learned, and where futures can still be changed.

Chapter 41

Strengthening Community Safeguards and Accountability

Creating a society where women and vulnerable groups feel safe requires more than institutional reforms; it necessitates the empowerment and active participation of communities themselves. Particularly in informal and marginalized settings, where oversight is minimal and exploitation can thrive, protective measures must be strengthened through registration, vigilance, education, and regulation. Women working in the unorganized sectors often face heightened risks of harassment and assault, made worse by the absence of formal protections. Ensuring safety in these contexts demands direct state involvement. Government authorities must conduct regular, unannounced inspections of labour sites that examine not only the condition of physical infrastructure but also the dynamics of interpersonal safety. Such visits can expose exploitative practices, detect warning signs of harassment or abuse, and ensure accountability for those who exploit the vulnerability of workers. Similarly, small establishments like repair shops, roadside eateries, and temporary sheds must not escape oversight. Registration and periodic monitoring can ensure that these spaces, often tucked away from scrutiny, do not become breeding grounds for predatory behaviour.

The brutal case of the Hyderabad veterinarian, who was assaulted and murdered near a roadside puncture shop, revealed in the most painful way the hidden dangers posed by unregulated and loosely monitored businesses. To prevent such tragedies, micro-enterprises such as puncture shops, mobile recharge centres, and roadside stalls should be mandatorily registered with local governing bodies, creating both a layer of accountability and a framework for corrective action when misconduct occurs. Alongside this, the mobility of transient and migratory populations, including daily wage workers, beggars, refugees, and the homeless, also calls for compassionate but structured registration systems. Done in ways that protect dignity and rights, such oversight contributes not only to community-level accountability but also to better resource planning and safety management.

Another crucial dimension of prevention lies in regulating data privacy and the misuse of personal information. In small tech service outlets and mobile recharge shops, workers often enjoy unrestricted access to people's phone numbers and other sensitive data, which can be easily abused for stalking, harassment, or blackmail. Holding shop owners to strict standards of data protection, and enforcing swift penalties for violations, is therefore essential. These businesses must also be monitored to prevent the circulation of pornographic content, particularly material that reaches minors or is forced upon vulnerable individuals. Regulatory bodies must treat harmful digital content as a serious threat to well-being and impose consequences accordingly.

Yet no amount of regulation can succeed without the strength of local participation. Community engagement is the backbone of sustainable safety, because protection becomes real only when it is shared. Grassroots leaders, such as members of village panchayats, must be included in training programs that equip them with knowledge on sexual violence prevention and survivor support. Once sensitized, such leaders can stand as the first line of defence and act as trusted points of contact within their communities. Similarly, neighbourhoods in high-risk areas should be empowered to form vigilance groups, not as instruments of fear or surveillance, but as immediate, responsive bodies that deter hostile behaviour and intervene when threats arise.

Technology too has a vital role. Mobile alerts, already used for cybercrime awareness, can be expanded to spread knowledge about consent, reporting mechanisms, child safety, and helpline access. Concise educational messages, delivered through SMS, local radio, or pre-recorded phone calls, can bridge barriers of geography and literacy, ensuring that essential information reaches even the remotest corners. By normalizing conversations on safety and rights, such interventions transform awareness into collective vigilance.

Beyond messaging, much can be achieved by mobilizing the people already embedded within communities. School teachers and Accredited Social Health Activists occupy positions of trust and contact in everyday life. With specialized training, they could recognize signs of abuse, offer initial support to survivors, and link them to proper services. They could also use structured checklists and referral mechanisms to identify individuals or environments at risk and trigger early interventions, turning grassroots workers into crucial protectors against violence.

All these measures point toward the same truth: safety cannot be left to the state alone. Lasting protection is possible only when state institutions enforce, but communities sustain, and individuals engage in the daily work of vigilance. This model is not about surveillance or suppression, but rather about nurturing responsibility where vulnerability is greatest. When knowledge, ethical conduct, and structured accountability take root within communities, they evolve from bystanders into guardians, and from passive spaces of risk into active ecosystems of care. To reimagine prevention in this way means embedding protection into the very fabric of society, not through fear but through participation, not by command but by shared responsibility. In such a society, safety ceases to be a privilege for the few and becomes a lived reality for all

Chapter 42

Bridging the Mental Health Gap: Professionals and Technology

The struggle against sexual violence is not merely a legal challenge or a social battle; it is also profoundly psychological. To address this crisis effectively, we must confront an overlooked but critical barrier: the country's vast mental health gap. On one side, India faces an acute shortage of psychiatrists, making specialized psychiatric care a scarce resource. On the other, the nation has produced a considerable number of trained psychologists who often face instability, underemployment, and lack of structured opportunities. This mismatch between scarcity and surplus is not just a structural inefficiency but also a signal that the system is failing both survivors and potential offenders. At the same time, it offers an unexpected opportunity: to reimagine the fight against sexual violence through the integration of mental health care into every layer of response and prevention.

One of the deepest impediments to such integration is cultural stigma. Mental health remains shrouded in silence, shame, and misconceptions. Seeking therapy is too often interpreted as an admission of weakness, while psychiatric consultations are clouded by fear of judgment or social ostracism. As a result, many victims of sexual violence never receive the psychological support they desperately need to process trauma, and many individuals at risk of perpetration are left without the interventions that might redirect harmful tendencies before they harden into violent behaviour. Breaking this cycle demands that mental health conversations become as ordinary and accepted as discussions on physical health. Nationwide campaigns that emphasize psychological support as a sign of strength rather than vulnerability could mark a critical cultural shift. Schools and universities, too, must normalize conversations about emotional wellbeing, preparing a generation that regards therapy and psychological care not with suspicion but with value and respect.

Addressing stigma alone is insufficient if access to care remains limited. India's psychiatrists are far too few for its population, and the burden they carry is overwhelming. Yet the country already possesses a large and underutilized workforce of psychologists whose skills remain on the margins of our institutional frameworks. By creating structured employment avenues for these professionals in schools, workplaces, primary health systems, and even law enforcement settings, we can tackle several challenges at once. Psychologists posted within schools could identify warning signs of victimization or aggressive tendencies among adolescents. Those embedded within hospitals could provide trauma-informed care to survivors immediately after assault. In workplaces, they could cultivate healthier environments while offering safe reporting mechanisms. Within police stations or legal systems, they could assess offender psychology and deliver interventions that reduce the risk of repeat offenses. In this way, psychologists become not peripheral actors but central to a proactive strategy that recognizes mental health as a frontline defence against sexual violence.

Transforming the role of psychologists also demands changes in how we educate professionals across disciplines. The academic approach to sexual violence in India often remains fragmented and outdated, leaving future lawyers, law enforcers, social workers, and healthcare providers poorly equipped to encounter the psychological complexities of this issue. Universities must go beyond legal frameworks or basic counselling courses and introduce comprehensive modules on criminal psychology with a focus on sexual crime, crime prevention, and behavioural intervention. Training should also include the study of victimology, enabling professionals to understand not only trauma but also the coping mechanisms, resilience pathways, and long-term mental health needs of survivors. Alongside this, curricula should push students to critically engage with the gaps in existing laws, support systems, and rehabilitation models, cultivating a workforce that is pragmatic, compassionate, and informed. Such reforms would ensure that professionals entering the system are trained not just in reacting, but in preventing, supporting, and ultimately transforming outcomes.

Any meaningful strategy must balance its focus on perpetrators with its commitment to survivors. While studying offender psychology helps us anticipate and prevent violence, equal investment is required in understanding survivors, their experiences of trauma, and their paths to recovery. Survivor-centric research is too often neglected, yet it can provide vital insights into how social support networks can be improved, how trauma persists or evolves, and which interventions enable individuals to rebuild their lives with dignity. Such research must always be conducted with stringent ethical safeguards, protecting privacy, ensuring informed consent, and maintaining dignity, so survivors are not retraumatized in the process. The data gathered can directly shape policies in law, healthcare, and education, aligning them more closely with the actual needs of survivors rather than abstract assumptions.

Technology introduces yet another critical dimension. In a society increasingly mediated by digital spaces, the risks of online exploitation, stalking, harassment, and grooming cannot be ignored. Cybercrime units must be given the capacity, resources, and specialized training to act with greater proactivity, intercepting misogynistic networks, explicit threats, or patterns of predatory behaviour before they find expression in the physical world. Social media platforms, with their vast influence, must refine algorithms that can flag abusive content and escalate high-risk behaviour for review. But prevention also lies in digital literacy: children and adolescents should be taught about online boundaries, privacy, and the mechanisms for reporting abuse, while parents and educators should be trained to recognize the often-subtle signs of digital exploitation. In this way, technology becomes not merely a channel through which harm occurs, but also an ally in prevention, vigilance, and accountability.

The psychological dimensions of sexual violence are complex, entrenched, and often invisible. Confronting them requires more than punitive statutes or incremental reforms. It demands that we build a robust mental health framework, expand spaces for psychologists, destigmatize therapy, reform educational systems, elevate research, and engage technology as a proactive tool. If mental health professionals are given structured roles, if curricula are modernized, if stigma is dismantled, and if digital vigilance is expanded, India can begin to move away from reactive adjustments toward proactive prevention. The convergence of psychological insight and technological advancement promises more than safety alone; it creates the foundations of a compassionate society that not only punishes acts of violence but also nurtures healing, prevents recurrence, and upholds the dignity of every individual. This is not merely a vision of reform but of transformation, of meeting violence at its source and disarming its roots with a combined force of empathy, science, and social will.

Chapter 43: A Medical Perspective on Prevention

This book approaches the issue of sexual violence through a medical lens, treating it as a societal condition that disproportionately impacts women and children, much in the same way that certain diseases such as systemic lupus erythematosus, uterine cancer, breast cancer, or retinoblastoma disproportionately affect these groups. The perpetrators of sexual violence are most often men, but the preventive strategies outlined here are not intended to dwell on blame. Instead, they focus on the safety and resilience of women and children, those who remain most vulnerable to harm and therefore most in need of protective frameworks.

This emphasis arises from an evolutionary and medical understanding of fear as a survival instinct. Fear has long been a companion to human life, a deeply rooted mechanism that helped our early ancestors detect danger and avoid predators on the savanna. In our modern world, where dangers are social rather than animal, this instinct still retains its purpose. It sharpens perception, guides choices, and can serve as a tool for anticipating harm before it manifests. Rather than pathologizing fear, this book explores its productive use in cultivating awareness and proactive prevention.

Medicine offers a useful analogy here. In preventing the spread of serious diseases, one of the very first strategies are avoiding the causative agent. When guarding against malaria or dengue, we advise individuals to avoid mosquito-prone areas or to take protective measures, not because mosquitoes define the entirety of the natural world, but because they can carry vectors of harm. In a similar sense, we can describe sexual violence in medical terms as a kind of social disease. Rapists are not equated to animals or pathogens in their humanity, but their behaviours function like vectors through which trauma is transmitted. Identifying patterns of harmful behaviour and incorporating safeguards against them follows the same preventive wisdom that medicine has long applied to other threats. Such analogies are not intended to stigmatize all men any more than public health warnings against mosquitoes suggest that every mosquito carries disease. They are ways of clarifying that vigilance, prudence, and situational awareness are necessary components of a protective strategy.

What is crucial to emphasize is that this analogy does not advocate a culture of restriction or fear, but rather a culture of awareness and empowerment. Just as vaccination, early detection, and education equip individuals against illnesses, situational awareness equips communities against the conditions that allow violence. The goal is not to cast women as perpetually endangered or helpless, but to give them tools, knowledge, and confidence to navigate risks where they emerge. Avoiding unsafe environments when warning signs are present, trusting instincts that flag vulnerability, and taking collective responsibility for safety can together function like preventative medicine at a societal level.

It is important to clarify that a medicalized model of understanding sexual violence must never be misinterpreted as victim-blaming or as an invitation to curtail women's freedoms. Any suggestion of such an interpretation stems only from the structural logic of applying a medical framework, which isolates causes, identifies risk, and proposes measures of prevention. In the same way that public health campaigns emphasize dietary precautions without blaming those affected by disease, this framework emphasizes awareness and vigilance without diminishing the fundamental rights, value, or dignity of women. Women should never be told to shrink their lives in the name of safety. Instead, society must provide the tools, policies, and systems that strengthen their ability to live fully, freely, and safely while recognizing the reality of risks that exist.

At its core, this approach is a call for systemic, evidence-based strategies rooted in both scientific insight and human compassion. It urges us to treat sexual violence not as an inevitable moral failing of individuals, but as a widespread condition that can be studied, managed, and mitigated when addressed with the same seriousness as a public health crisis. By combining prevention and awareness with survivor-cantered respect and early intervention, we move toward a society in which safety is not a privilege but a shared guarantee, and where the instinct of fear evolves not into limitation but into empowerment.

References For Further Studying:

Cohen, Marcia, and Sherrie H. McKenna. Rape: Psychology, Prevention and Impact. Routledge, 1979.

Encyclopedia of Violence, Peace, and Conflict. Edited by Lester R. Kurtz, Academic Press, 1999.

"In Interviews With 122 Rapists, Student Pursues Not-So-Simple Question: Why?" WBUR News, 22 Sept. 2010, www.wbur.org/news/2010/09/22/rapist-study.

Ellis, Lee, et al. "An Empirical Assessment of Some Feminist Hypotheses about Rape." International Journal of Law and Psychiatry, vol. 12, no. 3, 1989, pp. 403–419.

Greathouse, Sarah Michal, Jessica Saunders, Miriam Matthews, Kirsten M. Keller, and Laura L. Miller. "A Review of the Literature on Sexual Assault Perpetrator Characteristics and Behaviours." RAND Corporation, 2015.

"Characteristics of Male Perpetrators Who Sexually Assault Female Victims." RAND Corporation, 2015.

Lisak, David. "The Undetected Rapist." University of Massachusetts Boston, 2002.

Malamuth, Neil, Tamara Addison, and Mary Koss. "Pornography and Sexual Aggression: Are There Reliable Effects and Can Their Nature Be Determined?" Journal of Sex Research, vol. 27, no. 2, 1990, pp. 229–251.

Malamuth, Neil, Edward Heavey, and Edward Linz. "Predictors of Sexual Aggression in College Men: The Confluence Model of Sexual Aggression." Journal of Personality and Social Psychology, vol. 55, no. 5, 1993, pp. 953–963.

Malamuth, Neil, et al. "Sexual Aggression and the Confluence Model." Journal of Consulting and Clinical Psychology, vol. 59, no. 5, 1991, pp. 670–681.

Millett, Kate. Sexual Politics. Doubleday, 1970.

Palmer, Craig T. "Twelve Reasons Why Rape Is Not Sexually Motivated: A Skeptical Examination." Sexual Abuse: A Journal of Research and Treatment, vol. 3, no. 4, 1990, pp. 349–363.

Pandey, Madhumita. "Interviews with Men Convicted of Rape: Reflections and Lessons of a Female Researcher in a Male Delhi Prison." Feminism & Psychology, vol. 26, no. 4, 2016, pp. 451–469.

Sapolsky, Robert. Lectures. YouTube, uploaded

by Stanford University, 2010, www.youtube.com/playlist?list=PL848F2368C90DDC3D.

Scully, Diana. Understanding Sexual Violence: A Study of Convicted Rapists. Routledge, 1990.

Sleeman, William Henry. The Thugs or Phansigars of India. Oxford University Press, 1839.

Steidel, Yaeko. "Rapists and Their Parental Relationships." MA Thesis, Portland State University, 1979.

Sutherland, Edwin H. Principles of Criminology. 4th ed., J.B. Lippincott, 1947.

Thornhill, Randy, and Craig T. Palmer. "Why Do Men Rape? An Evolutionary Psychological Perspective." Review of General Psychology, vol. 11, no. 1, 2008, pp. 72–86.

"Types of Rape." Hope for Healing, archived on 5 Aug. 2012, archive.ph/2012.08.05-002413/http://www.hopeforhealing.org/types.html.

"Victimology." Encyclopedia of Victimology and Crime Prevention, edited by Bonnie S. Fisher and Steven P. Lab, SAGE Publications, 2010.

Acknowledgement

This book is the result of countless conversations, reflections, and courageous insights shared by many remarkable individuals. I am deeply grateful to each one of you.

Core Contributors and Pillars of Support

- **Umesh Tadasur (Psychologist):** What began as simple discussions after every brutal rape incident evolved into the foundation of this book. Your psychological insights, counseling anecdotes, and unwavering engagement—especially during the lockdown—have been the building blocks of this work.
- **Dr. Charu Smitha:** You have been the backbone of this project. From sharing the initial news to revising the draft, your support has been steadfast and invaluable.
- **Dr. Prof. Siddhaling Devaru:** Your immense help, thoughtful reviews, and encouragement—along with your foreword—have added depth and credibility to this work.

- **Sanjay Deodhar:** Your appreciation for every little adventure and misadventure of mine has been a constant source of encouragement.
- **Dr. Yogesh Rawal:** Your proud words after reviewing the manuscript meant a lot. Your insights on child sexual violence have been especially impactful.

Academic and Professional Guidance

- **Dr. Nikhil Saldhana, Dr. Nagaraj Lakshameshwar:** Your support and perspectives have been unforgettable.
- **Dr. Manjunath Sharma, Dr. Vinutha, Dr. Suguna, Dr. Guruprasad:** Your experiences from Gynaec OPDs, especially regarding perverted patients and their attendants, have served as critical evidence in understanding perversion.
- **Dr. (Prof.) Varsha Mokashi (HOD, Anatomy):** Your insights into human anatomical evolution have contributed significantly.
- **Dr. (Prof.) Saroja RK (HOD):** Thank you for your appreciation and HOD, Radio diagnosis/Nuclear Medicine for a book of this nature.

Literary and Editorial Support

- **Rishikesh Bahadur Desai:** Your advice to keep the book non-scientific was well taken. Your inputs on statistics, NCRB data, and news sources were instrumental.
- **Mahesh KN (Frankfurt):** Grateful for your everlasting love for literature, intelligent discussions,

and Doner kebaps.

- **Dr. Smile, Imam Nadaf, Ismail Nadaf:** Thank you for your efforts in finding a publisher and providing reviews.
- **Dr. Laxman Atpatkar, Yogesh Master, Dr. Riyaz Ahmed Bode:** Your sincere appreciation and connections have been pillars of support.

Friends, Family, and Unnamed Contributors

My **MBBS batch buddies** and **chuddi buddies:**
Rajkumar (Perth), Dr. Suresh Wagh, Suresh (Toyota), Pachaxayya Hiremath (Indian Railways)—your pride and encouragement have always lifted me.
My wife and kids: Thank you for letting me write in peace and for your silent strength.
The **British Noble Press** team and all those who contributed anonymously with data, personal opinions, and views on rape and its causes—your courage and honesty are deeply appreciated.

Media and Research Sources

Thanks to the newspapers, websites, adult sites, AI platforms, and all researchers and scientific workers who have pioneered work on rape mentality. Your contributions have helped shape the understanding of this issue from a health and psychological perspective.

www.ingramcontent.com/pod-product-compliance
Lightning Source LLC
Chambersburg PA
CBHW050013170726
48282CB00025B/381
9789373158204